MAN AND METAPHYSICS

IS VOLUME

35

OF THE

Twentieth Century Encyclopedia of Catholicism

UNDER SECTION

III

THE NATURE OF MAN

IT IS ALSO THE

71ST

VOLUME IN ORDER OF PUBLICATION

Edited by *HENRI DANIEL-ROPS* of the *Académie Française*

MAN AND METAPHYSICS

By RÉGIS JOLIVET

Translated from the French by B. M. G. REARDON

HAWTHORN BOOKS · PUBLISHERS · *New York*

First Edition, August, 1961
Second Printing, May, 1964

NIHIL OBSTAT

Joannes M. T. Barton, S.T.D., L.S.S.

Censor deputatus

IMPRIMATUR

E. Morrogh Bernard

Vicarius Generalis

Westmonasterii, die XIII MAII, MCMLXI

H-9497

CONTENTS

THE PLANES OF KNOWLEDGE

Knowledge is multiform. The history of man as a "thinking animal" shows in the plainest possible manner that the understanding is developed and realized in a diversity of ways seemingly quite distinct from one another, so that no one of them has any right or title to disqualify the rest. It would even appear that man never ceases to use them all simultaneously and that he cannot reject any of them without at the same time excluding the others. Thus the kind of reasoning which would banish intuition is self-destructive, and *vice versa*. Descartes, following St Augustine, declares that the geometer or the mathematician could never have laid a true foundation for his discipline, however rigorous it may be at its own level, without recourse to metaphysics in the form of an affirmation of the existence of God as the *locus* or creator of the eternal verities. In the same way, and despite the enormous successes which they have achieved, the sciences of nature, so far from confirming the positivist doctrine which would set them up as the type of all science, have increasingly revealed to scientific thinkers themselves that in the last resort they are incapable of really fulfilling that grand ambition of *knowing* which is the characteristic of our humanity. Do what you will, yet always on the horizons of positive knowledge stands metaphysics. Moreover, there are ways of knowing, to be described as "poetical" and "mystical", which it is

impossible to deny without injuring or denying reason itself
—in any case without assuming, gratuitously and arbitrarily,
that knowledge is *univocal*,* and thus countering the most
persistent experience of the human race.

The term "positive knowledge", often referred nowadays
to the natural sciences and in particular to physics, really
denotes, when one comes to consider it, less a fact than a
theory, implicit at least and certainly highly contestable, since
it takes for granted that there is only one sort of "positivity".
The truth indeed is that all knowledge worthy of the name
must be *positive*; that is to say, founded on *experience*. But
there are many different ways of being "positive": in other
words, many and differing possibilities of experience. *Sensible*
experience, at the common-sense level, is one of these; and,
in fact, all knowledge may be said to derive, in one respect or
another, from experience of this sort, as in our day Edmund
Husserl (taking his cue from Aristotle) has clearly shown;
even though, contrary to what empiricists* are wont to tell
us, it cannot be wholly accounted for on that basis alone.
The natural sciences certainly are entirely dependent on sense-
experience, while also being limited by it. There is, too, an
experience which may be called *metempirical** and which im-
parts to knowledge, prior to any technical elaboration of it,
the fundamental patterns of the phenomenal world in the
form of *schemata* embodying elements both of representation
and of interpretation. Experience of this order, however, is as
a rule bound up with that of sense and is to be distinguished
from it only by abstraction. On a still higher plane, *metaphysical* experience is the comprehension, within reality itself
and under a form which is wholly proper to it, of the first
principles of the real. Thus perception, the apprehension of
categories* and the grasp of supra-sensible first principles are

---

* It is impossible to treat of metaphysics without employing a certain number of technical terms. The essential thing is to define them
with sufficient precision. Such definitions are supplied in a short
glossary at the end of this book. They are indicated, as they occur, by
an asterisk.

all equally "positive", though not necessarily after the same manner. It might also be said that one can have a "poetic" experience which, though itself "positive", would nevertheless imply yet another plane of knowledge. And the same could even be said of *mystical* experience, which is ultimate and irreducible.

But here we encounter many more problems than we do solutions. If the history of thought shows that common sense, experimental science (at least in a rudimentary way), met-empiricism and metaphysics have always co-existed and mutually supported one another, it is no less full of inquiries, arguments and disputes about the relative value of these diverse experiences. Metaphysics in particular has met with objections which cast doubt upon its genuineness as a mode of knowledge. It is not enough therefore to maintain that differing modes of knowledge have always co-existed, or that Auguste Comte, who dismissed all metaphysics as bogus, was actually one of the great metaphysicians of his century. The problem must be approached on the speculative level, where the arguments of philosophers have placed it.

To this end our task will comprise, first, a phenomenological definition and analysis, and if possible a justification, of what may be called *metaphysical experience*; and then, arising from such analysis, a statement of the most important problems that make up the content of metaphysics *as a science*.

PART I

METAPHYSICAL EXPERIENCE

Man has often been defined as a *metaphysical animal*, which, though doubtless telling us no more than that he is a "reasoning animal", at least indicates the characteristic power of reason: that of looking beyond the empirical and relative to the "absolute". "The ideas of Being, of the Absolute and of Reality", says a modern philosopher, Edouard Le Roy, "are the centre and foundation of all metaphysics"; and again, "The whole tradition of metaphysical thought understands by metaphysical truth possession by the mind of Reality, of the Absolute and of Being".[1] Man therefore, from this standpoint, is of his very essence metaphysical; which means that there is in him something incapable of expression in terms simply of "nature", or *physis*: something which always radically transcends nature and which is to be described as *spirit*. The ancients emphasized this by saying that man, by reason of what is spiritual in him, both in his knowledge and in his being is an *addition* to nature: *Homo additus naturae*.

This, however, has been disputed; and the doctrines known as materialism, empiricism and positivism have denied his metaphysical character, or at least have sought to reduce it to pure illusion. We shall have to examine their arguments in due course. But we can note at once that if the metaphysical in man is illusory, at all events the illusion itself is real enough and constitutes, as we say nowadays, a phenomenon or group of phenomena which must at the outset be scientifically established and correctly described. That will be our aim in the following three chapters.

[1] *Philosophie première* (Paris, 1956) I, p. 121.

CHAPTER I

THE FACT OF
METAPHYSICS

DEFINITIONS

For a definition of what metaphysics is we could perhaps go first to history. We should then discover that the term "metaphysics" carries with it a wide range of meanings: it is the science of the non-material, of the real-in-itself, of the unknowable, of the absolute; a systematic universal knowledge, *a priori* knowledge, and so forth. All these definitions in fact hold good—from a given standpoint. But that is their weakness; they are too partial. Aristotle spoke of metaphysics, more accurately, as the *science of being* qua *being*—a definition which seems to correspond more fully, in virtue of its generality, with the progress and natural rhythm of knowledge, and to be justified by its synthetic character, since it covers all that is positive in the other definitions which we have instanced.

The science of being *qua* being is indeed the science of the *non-sensible*, or the *non-material*, though we cannot at the outset anticipate more than the possibility of beings that are positively non-material. The science of being is also that of the *real-in-itself*, since in treating of being it deals with that which is most real, inasmuch as being is the condition of all reality. Again, it is the science of the *unknowable*, so far at least as its object, as we shall see, is not *an object*; for it wholly transcends sense-experience and cannot be known for what it is in itself—which is why we must resort to the method of analogy*. Yet again, the science of being is the science of the *absolute*, in so far as (*a*) being is the absolute of all existents (i.e. of individual, concrete beings), and (*b*) it seeks to define the causes and absolutely first principles of the universe. Further, metaphysics is *systematic universal knowledge* because the standpoint of being as such is the most highly synthetic of all, since everything is defined, judged and explained in relation to being. Finally, it can be regarded as an *a priori* knowledge in the sense that the idea of being is itself the *a priori* condition of all knowing.

Thus the definition of metaphysics as the *science of being* is both the most genuinely comprehensive and the most illuminating, since it is in being—or, preferably perhaps, on the basis of being—that the successive stages of a philosophy which seeks an ultimate interpretation of man and the universe become possible. And it is because metaphysical philosophy has as object the whole of our experience of being that it lacks *an* object, unlike the special sciences, which cannot be formally defined without reference to a particular subject-matter, however general this may be. The definition of metaphysics as the science of being is therefore the most appropriate to the breadth and universality of its scope, which, in comprising all things, is to be identified neither with a single object nor with the sum of all objects, but is that by which every object, actual or possible, acquires a meaning and so becomes the subject of an affirmation which recognizes it as being the particular thing which it is.

Heidegger, in our day, adopts essentially the same standpoint, but insists on the fact that the question of being— which is what metaphysics is—becomes itself *a mode of being for the questioner*. It is a case, we may say, of the existent in all of us questioning himself about the being of existence. "No metaphysical question", he says, "can be asked without at the same time the questioner himself being included in the question." Gabriel Marcel, too, has often pointed out how metaphysics has this character; so much so indeed that, by the mere fact of our existing we are already up to our eyes in metaphysics! It is our nature to be metaphysical. That is why metaphysics, as Heidegger again insists, is of such importance; no other science, no matter how rigorous its methods, can equal it. So also Sartre: "Metaphysics is not just a sterile discussion of abstract notions lying outside experience, but", he contends, "a vital attempt to embrace from within the human condition in its totality"[1] and to resolve, as far as possible, the basic question of "the existence of the existent".[2]

No doubt we could say of these definitions that they prejudge the issue, as they themselves presuppose metaphysical doctrines of one kind or another. In reckoning with this objection we shall have to tackle the problem pretty well from its beginnings, setting out from a nominal definition on which all philosophers could agree; a definition which would really be no more than a description of the metaphysical phenomenon. Such a phenomenological analysis would of course bypass the question whether man's metaphysical aspirations are well-founded or not. It would simply serve to show what it is that we are talking about, without involving us in any dialectical subtleties.

OUR "METAPHYSICAL NEED"

The etymology of the word "metaphysics" tells us practically all we want to know about it. The term was first used to denote those works of Aristotle which, in the collection of Andronicus of Rhodes, were placed *after* "Physics" (or natural philosophy); but it has come to signify "what is beyond the physical" and hence connotes a certain knowledge of, or capacity for knowing, supra-sensible reality, so giving birth to a systematic understanding of things which transcend

[1] J.-P. Sartre, *Situations* (Paris 1948) II, p. 251.
[2] J.-P. Sartre, *L'Être et le Néant*, p. 354.

the visible world, an understanding, that is, which is essentially *transphysical*.

If anything is certain in the history of man as a thinking being it is this universal aim of his, under the conditions of time and space, of extending his knowledge beyond the realm of the purely "given" and of entering that of the invisible and transcendent. However crude the images and representations may be which man has made for himself of this invisible, supra-sensible world, we must recognize, across the centuries, a continuous and untiring effort on his part to thrust out beyond mere appearance, beyond phenomena, in quest of a non-material universe, a "first principle" of all things, an absolute truth. There is even an implicit metaphysic in myth itself.

This whole attempt seems to spring from the very spontaneity of man's reason and to have been made, in the first instance, quite without effort. As Émile Meyerson tells us, "man practises metaphysics just as he breathes, without thinking about it". In fact, no criticism of this spontaneous play of mind was undertaken until fairly late in the history of thought, when man, turning his reflection upon himself, tried to find grounds for the metaphysical activity which he at first indulged in altogether naturally. The human mind follows its native bent and concerns itself only subsequently, and then somewhat hesitatingly, with the forms of what, to begin with, was a simple and quite unreflecting exercise. When, however, man does start to reflect systematically, technically and critically it is not and cannot be upon any other object than the vital experience of life at its concrete level.

Let us attempt, then, an analysis of the differing forms of what Schopenhauer called "man's metaphysical need". We shall keep to the plane of phenomena as seen in their simplest objectivity and regardless of what their real basis may be—an inquiry to which we shall return later.

Analysis, when applied to what we may describe as man's natural and spontaneous metaphysical impulse, discovers at its source an aspiration, a need, a demand—call it what you will; such terms in any case will have to be clarified—that can be characterized by the two words *infinite* and *absolute*. Placed in—or pitched into—a world which, by its sheer immensity, overwhelms him without at the same time satisfying him, confronted with which his feelings are at once those of astonishment, admiration and disquiet, man would appear to be moved by a kind of craving for the infinite; or, more precisely, by an infinite dynamism which continually drives him beyond what he sees, grasps or imagines—though as yet without any assignable goal. In this sense, however, the infinite is less the term of an unending movement towards a future ever open than the power to go on questioning, as either insufficient, precarious or limited, every actual attainment or value. The infinite, as Descartes perceived, is present in the power to test and question all finitude, a power not always explicit, indeed, but rather lived and developed both in the effort to discover what, of itself, is without limits—in man's constant awareness of his inability to find on earth a resting-place equal to the range and depth of his longings—and ultimately in the protest of conscience at the facts of suffering and death. Kierkegaard held that "the existential thinker" should be a man of "pathos" (or disquiet) and that he should feel himself to be always alone "above six thousand fathoms of water". The truth is—though academic philosophers, in making "a good thing" out of their metaphysical systems, succeed only in missing the sheer wonder of existence, the sheer anguish of freedom—that the plain man, at least at moments, does experience the uncertainty and precariousness of his condition and feel himself veritably tossed about "above more than six thousand fathoms of water", conscious as he is of being "suspended on the verge of nothingness". The various romantic guises which man's longing for the infinite has assumed—and which certainly are no small incentive to eloquence—must not be allowed to mask what seems to be really deep, essential and intrinsic in our human finitude, as we perhaps may term it.

This, then, can be said quite simply: all the indications are that man is a being ill at ease who has always been impelled beyond himself—beyond, that is, his condition as a natural creature—towards a transcendent reality, often ill-defined and difficult enough to define, which nevertheless is fundamentally, at least when its full implications are grasped, a negation of all limitations and hence even of the finite world of appearances. As Rodrigue exclaims in Claudel's *Le Soulier de Satin*: "There is a prison we have had enough of! There are these eyes which have a right to see the end of things! There is a heart which cries out for satisfaction!" The experience of happiness, even when cut short by suffering and death, has always been for mankind an anticipation of the transcendent, since although it is certain that man has known no other happiness than one which is fleeting, chequered and incomplete, he yet has not ceased to feel that of its very essence it *ought* to be eternal. Whether this need of the infinite (or of the eternal)—the impulse towards it or the attraction of it—is an illusion is a question to be examined. At all events it is a constant fact which no analysis of our humanity may overlook. Descartes based his whole metaphysical system upon it, centring it, as is well known, on the idea of perfect (or infinite) being, inscribed, as he claimed, at the very heart of our finite existence and impossible to explain either by what we are or by what we acquire in experience.

These views are fundamental also to Maurice Blondel's "philosophy of action". They arise, he states, from a method which seeks "to balance within consciousness itself whatever we appear to think and intend to do with what we actually do and intend and think, in such a way that our factitious denials and artificially willed ends reveal the profound affirmations and unshakable needs which they imply".[3] It is a

[3] See M. Blondel, *L'Action* (1893), pp. 467–74.

method which is plainly that of a realist philosophy, applied, in opposition to an unrealistic and abstract conception of man, to one that is quite realist and concrete. For man is self-revealed in and by action, which is the permanent principle of unity within us. However divided and rent we may be by our internal contradictions, yet it is in and by action that we succeed in unifying these divisions; since action tends to an end, and this end expresses us and gives us the meaning, declared or hidden, of our deepest being. Now an analysis of will shows that its scope is utterly unlimited, for were it to engulf the whole world it still would not be satiated, its capacity exceeding each and every act in which it finds expression. Thus it is that man reached the idea of the infinite: the will being impossible to satisfy with finite things, it seems that the infinite alone can meet its longings. Clearly, then, the idea of the infinite is not the result of simple, abstract analysis or arbitrary decision, but, on the contrary, is really all the time present in the will itself. We do not therefore have to solve a metaphysical problem in order to "live" metaphysics.[4]

It is the positive aspect of this idea of infinity which, when considered both speculatively and morally, gives rise to the concept of God. Hence in all of us there is a desire of the infinite (inherent in the will's own dynamism); and together with this and uniting with it, a *desire of God*, a desire for God to exist, which itself implies an aspiration (though it cannot be precisely defined apart from Revelation) towards divinity. We shall see how metaphysics, as a science, must in the last resort be regarded as a deliberate recognition or critical articulation of this metaphysical *datum* as something intrinsic to the natural spontaneity of man's basic will when understood in terms of its highest ambition.

From the standpoint of reason such an aspiration is to be seen as a demand for the *absolute*. "The whole secret of method," Descartes tells us, "consists in the careful search for

[4] *Op. cit.*, p. 353.

what in everything most nearly approaches the absolute."[5] But before becoming a method and a system this same demand is, we realize, something that lies at the root of our intellectual being. It embodies the instinctive feeling that, in every order of reality, there must be some primary term as the condition of all others and, as such, independent—as the etymology of the word "ab-solute" itself shows—at least in its own order. More, it suggests, however confusedly, that beyond all the orders of being, as also beyond all the relative "absolutes" which dominate them, there is a principle or source of order transcending all that it creates (or more precisely, calls into self-creating existence), which on that account must be designated *the* Absolute, in the truest sense of the word.

This demand for intelligibility* is expressed in every form of human thought, from the lowest—the mythological and the crudely pictorial—to the highest and purest. The idea of God, with its universality, is the most comprehensive answer we can give to the question of the absolute. For God is the Absolute *par excellence*, absolute in his independence of all that is or can be. All other absolutes—the first principles, that is, of the many and various orders of reality which thought believes itself to have discovered in the age-long course of its reflective activity—appear only as relative-absolutes which, in turn, on account of their relativity and consequent dependence, call for a perfect and wholly non-relative Absolute sufficient to explain their own nature and being.

It is certainly true that this search for the sole Absolute has given rise in the course of history to a good many conceptions which reflection has been obliged to reject or at least to correct. As Schopenhauer observes, an aptitude for metaphysics is not necessarily coincident with a sense of metaphysical need. But such aberrations are themselves significant as pointers to a tendency which seems to be native to the human spirit. As such they yet can be of help in defining, as

[5] *Règles pour la direction de l'esprit*, VI.

regards what is really essential and permanent, the true direction of thought. We shall see that much modern philosophy, in disputing man's ability to discover any "absolute" of thought or of being—when not indeed denying outright the very possibility of such an absolute—has merely transferred to the world of experience that quality of absoluteness which the mind, when following its first spontaneous impulse, attributed to transphysical realities. The whole of human history is evidence of how man is never in fact without an absolute and how the real problem becomes one of correctly defining the nature and the meaning of something which reason itself is tireless in seeking and invoking.

MAN'S "RATIONAL INSTINCT" AND THE FACT OF RELIGION

The phenomenon of metaphysics has still other aspects, which we may call "subjective", in contrast with the foregoing, which have to do with reality, or, more precisely, with the "objective" world of man's experience or basic purposiveness. This indeed is always recognized as involving three orders of value—reason, liberty and morality—which distinguish it from nature and constitute it as a realm of its own. It has been possible, on the theory of evolution, to envisage a progressive emergence of humanity from the animal world, either continuously or through successive mutations. With this argument we need not concern ourselves here. But, even conceding its truth, it remains that man as such does not come into being until the moment (and in the measure) of his endowment with the capacity for rational thought, however embryonic; with the capacity, that is, for self-determination and the reflective choice of his own actions, and eventually for obedience to the moral imperative. In this last domain the moral experience of guilt, so it has been noted, is formally of the order of metaphysical experience, since it implies, beyond any mere feeling, that a law has been broken. It denotes, in fact, a sense of responsibility: "The judgement which I pass upon myself is identical with one which an absolute Conscience would make", a relationship, in other words, "of the self to the God who dwells within it".[6]

It is all this that is implied in the description of man as *homo sapiens*, the epithet *sapiens* covering at once his reason, his freedom and his sense of moral values, and carrying with it the idea of a "metaphysical light" intended to shed its rays both throughout the entire universe of "things" and upon every activity of the human mind. However far back we go into the night of prehistory, it is certain that man buries his dead, thus disclosing a kind of faith in his own transcendence and in the immortality of the spiritual principle (called by analogy "breath") which animates him. The prehistoric cave-paintings which often display so high an artistic development, reveal, along with the influence of magic—which can well appear as a degradation of man's spiritual sense—a profound capacity for contemplating nature and, by thus dominating it, for gaining freedom from it. The whole being of metaphysical man is already present in this movement from nature to consciousness and liberty. Accordingly, the meaning of civilization will be, in the course of the ages, to create and bring to perfection means ever more numerous and effective of realizing the full implications of this primal expression of man's autonomy. That is why civilization itself is metaphysical in its essence.

Doctrines which seek to minimize the significance of these characteristically human values by representing them as illusions devoid of any real basis forget that, as Karl Marx justly observed, "the only questions [*enigmas* is his word] which humanity raises are those which it can answer". These questions consistently testify to the reality and permanence of the human phenomenon as a metaphysical one. For these three basic values establish man as a being apart in the world, a being essentially transcending the entire physical order. As we already have noted, reason turns spontaneously

[6] J. Nabert, *Éléments pour une Éthique* (Paris, 1943), p. 13.

towards what lies beyond the world. For thought's most constant exercise is in the realm of the universal; the mind aspires to unity with what is absolute, and above all with an Absolute which is ultimate and supreme and which, of its very nature, is accessible to mind alone. Freedom in its turn is affirmed in the activity of thought by which man, debating within himself the range of possibilities offered to his choice, escapes from his physical limitations and comes to regard himself as the architect of his own destiny. Finally, morality, even when hardly as yet distinguishable from social constraint, imposes duties and obligations which imply the reality of another world than that of "fact": a world, namely, which is moral and spiritual and irreducible to that of mere objects, and by which, despite risk and pain, man achieves his own truest dignity.

Thus it is that he appears as a metaphysical being: by all that marks him out from the rest of the world which he inhabits he out-tops the whole universe of sense. It would seem to be little or no exaggeration to speak here of an instinct which is quite specifically human, over and above those that belong to man's animal nature—the alimentary, the sexual, the gregarious—which themselves are radically transformed when associated with reason. This specifically human instinct, the purpose of which is to control and guide the others, may indeed be called the *rational*, the threefold object of which is the discovery of truth and the acquisition of knowledge; the realization of the good in the freedom of the moral life; and the creation of beauty in works of art. For all these activities have their roots in the reason, of which they are the endlessly varied and complex expressions, as natural and as universal as is the latter itself. They emerge spontaneously, in the child as in the "primitive" and the savage. Man's remotest prehistory already bears unmistakable witness to their presence. Education and the progress of civilization—itself a product of the rational instinct—do but multiply and diversify unceasingly the means of its articulation.

The universality of the *fact of religion* in space and time—a fact which is part and parcel of that demand for the absolute which we have analysed above—is in its turn one of the clearest and most striking expressions of man's metaphysical character. Indeed it is in religion that the metaphysical demand for the absolute always assumes concrete form, less from any speculative necessity (however implicit) than from the practical one that the moral consciousness seeks the divine. What is called "rational theology" develops only within the shadow of religion, from which, for the average man, it is indistinguishable except by an effort of abstraction more or less difficult. The absolute of the metaphysicians, legitimate though it may be for the purpose and within the limits of such abstraction, always has a "secular" air about it, so that we tend as a rule to refer somewhat pejoratively to "the God of the philosophers and the scientists". Newman well said that "the philosopher aspires to a divine *principle*, the Christian towards a divine *Agent*".[7] That is why the deism beloved of Voltaire and Lessing seems such an absurd and bloodless thing; why, too, philosophical theism maintains itself, in practice if not in theory—a point Pascal made against Descartes[8]—only by the hidden aid of a religious belief, apart from which it becomes a mere intellectual notion, a frigid theorem. Finally, it explains why atheism, which also is to be met with in history—though in a systematic form which indicates that it is of late and even accidental occurrence—is itself a proof, by reason of its invariably polemical character (witness Lucretius in antiquity, or Nietzsche and Marx in the modern world), of the reality and depth of the religious impulse.

It seems—to view that matter at its purely phenomenal level—that in separating himself from all religion man fails to arrive at a true self-understanding and that he divests

[7] *University Sermons*, p. 29. A divine *Subject* would perhaps have been better.

[8] Cf. Pascal, *Pensées* (ed. Brunschvicg), pp. 142, Mémorial, 545.

himself of his metaphysical character only at the cost of denying his essential humanity. Moreover, it is evident that on the ruins of supernatural religion other faiths—religions of Science, of Progress, of Humanity, of History—are built up which substitute for God or the gods of the historic religions new and *ersatz* divinities, designed to meet that craving of man's reason for an absolute which in some form or other it can never do without. As Brunetière used to say: "If you don't believe in Spirit you will believe in Matter—and in spirits under the counter!"[9] This, however, need not be enlarged on here. Our present purpose is simply to describe and analyse the main features of that metaphysical propensity which from his earliest origins has ever been man's distinctive characteristic.

NATURAL METAPHYSICS

We are faced, then, by a fact, the most certain and universal of any, as Kant himself admitted when he wrote:

> In a certain sense this kind of knowledge must unquestionably be looked upon as *given*; in other words, metaphysics must be considered as really existing, if not as a science, nevertheless as a natural disposition of the human mind (*metaphysica naturalis*).

And he adds:

> Human reason, without any instigations imputable to the mere variety of great knowledge, unceasingly progresses, urged on by its own feeling of need, towards such questions as cannot be answered by any empirical application of reason, or principles derived therefrom; and so there has ever really existed in every man some system of metaphysics. It always will exist, so soon as reason awakes to the exercise of its power of speculation.[10]

[9] F. Brunetière, *Discours de combat* (Le besoin de croire) (Paris, 1908) III, p. 309.
[10] *Critique of Pure Reason*, trans. J. M. D. Meiklejohn, pp. 13–14.

Metaphysics as a science has its foundation in a spontaneous cognitive activity which, although itself pre-scientific, is nonetheless metaphysical in character. So much is plain fact. It remains, however, to explain it; to do this is the task of philosophy.

If Kant is right in saying that metaphysics is the outcome of a "natural disposition", expressing itself in the form of an inevitable *question* about being and man, so that it springs from the very nature of the rational understanding, we may go on to ask how it is that this question is both possible and necessary; and thence to examine the capacity of man as a thinker and to inquire whether the reason has its grounds in the assurance that he can in fact answer it; in other words, whether metaphysics can in all strictness be called a *science*.

We must admit, however, that all this is rather abstract and suggests that we are so much at home with the idea of metaphysics as to forget that it is itself a mystery. That metaphysics is the child of wonder and that man, as Schopenhauer says, is "the only animal who wonders at his own existence" or who asks himself what in truth he is,[11] or, still more comprehensively, wonders at the sheer givenness of existence or being—even this, despite anything Kant may suggest, is not simply to be taken for granted but ought rather itself to be a prime cause of wonder. For in the end everything seems to be related to everything else within a single continuant cosmos. Nothing is more natural, more obvious, than existence. Is there anything, among phenomena, which leads us to think of it as a purely gratuitous occurrence miraculously renewed from moment to moment, any more than there is to favour the Cartesian hypothesis of a world made up of discrete moments or atomic points for ever being destroyed by their own weight only to be re-created again by an absolutely free

---

[11] Schopenhauer but repeats the words of Plato, that "wonder is, of all others, the truly philosophical feeling" (*Theaetetus*, 155 D); as also of Aristotle: "It is by wonder that men, now as at the beginning, have first begun to philosophize" (*Metaphysics*, A 2, 982a).

act, so that all things, in truth, exist only by virtue of an unceasing miracle? Death no doubt appears to cause a certain disorder, but the disorder is not specific, since the species continues to maintain itself and thus is in a way eternal, as Aristotle points out; nor is it cosmic, since it is no more than an accident, a mere wrinkle on the surface of being which yet has some part to play in the universal process. As a purely individual episode, the sense of the consistent wholeness of things deprives it of all appearance of tragedy. "Footprints in the snow. Writing on the sands. A phosphorescent gleam, lost for ever in the blackness of the ocean. Someone has lived (without having asked to), has suffered, and then has disappeared—and nothing remains beyond a handful of chemical substances and a 'tomb without a name'."[12] Why, then, sigh and protest? Life carries on without interruption, feeding even on death itself. What is there to be astonished at? The machine never breaks down.

Yet, in spite of all, man does wonder and worry and question himself endlessly—and about that precisely which, to all appearance, raises no real problem. "Let nought surprise thee", says Marcus Aurelius, with the accumulated wisdom of the Stoa behind him. For the wind will scatter it away! This passion of wonder in which Plato finds the germ of the philosophic vocation, this "wonder at existence" (as he calls it) by which, of a sudden, the familiar world around us collapses under the searcher's gaze, already proclaims for us the nature of man as man, in so far at least as he is free of the domination of his merely biological impulses. The philosopher's task is to explain and analyse it; but to begin with he observes how it springs from his humanity itself, and above all from the gnawing fear, more spiritual than physical, of death.

Such, then, is the enigma of man's being and the anxiety which possesses him. To say that nothing is more natural is insufficient to explain either of them; for they certainly are

[12] V. Jankelevitch, *Philosophie première* (Paris, 1954), p. 247.

not "natural". They ought, rather, to be called "supernatural". Subjectively speaking, it is because of them that man at once fulfils and transcends himself. That is why he is metaphysical. On the other hand, when viewed objectively, this feeling of wonder, in all the forms which it assumes—admiration, disquiet, anxiety, stupefaction, giving rise as they do to endless questionings—appears as an awareness of the "mystery" in which we are involved and which man tries to encompass by means of three queries: What are we? Whence do we come? Whither are we bound?; or else by the more general and comprehensive question of being and its ultimate significance.[13] For man, as Plotinus states, is never content merely to contemplate the brilliance of the stars, the splendour of the heavens and the beauty of the earth; by the same impulse his thoughts turn to their Author, and indeed still further, to that which is no longer simply to be marvelled at but which constitutes the mystery underlying all marvels—namely, the One.[14] So, in that fleeting moment of illumination when he glimpses the truth about himself, and by a paradox wherein the whole majesty of consciousness resides, man sees himself as possessing powers of wonder and boundless contemplation; and marvels, in turn, how it is that he should thus be a consciousness which, in reaching out towards its source, is capable of transcending the very being of which it is conscious, while at the same time remaining immanent therein; just as, according to Pascal, the thinking reed, as something that exists, itself thinks the existence which it manifests, and as "thought conceives of existence in general as an abstraction which produces vertigo", while bearing witness to the given in virtue of its own existence.[15]

[13] Plato, who justly observed that "wonder" is the characteristic philosophical emotion, notes also (*Republic*, Book IV) that "the masses are incapable of philosophizing". But this is true only so far as concerns metaphysics *as a science*, since every man is a natural metaphysician from the very fact of his humanity, which is inherently metaphysical.

[14] *Enneads*, III, 8, 11; VI, 9, 5.

[15] V. Jankelevitch, *Philosophie première*, p. 176.

CHAPTER II

THE MEANING AND SCOPE
OF THE METAPHYSICAL
PHENOMENON

Nevertheless, all that we have just been saying with regard to the bare fact of the metaphysical phenomenon counts for little or nothing in the eyes of many modern philosophers. For them it is an illusion only, "pure ontological imagination," as Léon Brunschvicg puts it. Kant himself who, in the very passage we have cited, attributes man's metaphysical interest to a "natural disposition", denies that metaphysics can legitimately claim to be a science: a systematic knowledge, that is, based on objective principles admitting of no challenge. Questions, he tells us, which are put to us by the reason "cannot be answered by any empirical application of reason, or by principles derived therefrom". The whole positivist way of thinking follows much the same line, even more boldly, perhaps, and with less perception—for what Kant refused to "reason" he restored to "belief". All such arguments need to be examined. We shall dwell on them, however, only briefly and by way of a more systematic analysis of what we mean by the "metaphysical phenomenon", in the hope of discovering both its most general form and its true basis.

THE QUESTION OF BEING

At first glance the universe presents itself to us as a source of unlimited fertility, an endless outpouring of "things" or concrete beings. Faced with this abundance and with a world which, in some manner, fashions it into a "whole", we quite spontaneously and irresistibly put the question: What is all this? In the first instance it is the necessities of life which move us to say that things are such and such—of this or that kind (a tree, a metal, of water or of air, living, etc.), and thereafter to frame definitions of them—not, it may be, with any particular care for scientific accuracy, but simply to state *what they are*.

Yet this is not enough; for it is clear that the "essence" or "nature" of a thing is not an arbitrary invention but belongs to the "givenness" of reality. It is in fact its objectivity which most immediately strikes us. Any criticism of this objectivity —for example, by exposing "errors of the senses" or by reducing the qualities which the senses apprehend (colour, sound, smell, heat and so on) to mere motions—is a much later step, and although it can induce us to modify or even transform the concept of objectivity itself it will in no way destroy our conviction of the reality of things or beings as independent of the knower. Things *are*; they are inherently part of *being*. But at the same time they raise, as such, a problem which is already intrinsically metaphysical: that, namely, of their *raison d'être*—the grounds alike of the *concrete reality* which they are (their "essences") and of the *being* which they share (their "existence").

It may well of course be asked whether such a question is meaningful and whether such grounds can be demonstrated. But what at any rate can be said at this juncture, without in any way prejudicing an explanation to be given later, is that the very fact of posing the question of being in itself implies a certain *experience of being*, apart from which the actual question would be incomprehensible and most likely never asked. Heidegger, in our day, has repeatedly stressed this and we can rely on his analysis. It consists in showing—since here it is strictly a matter of *seeing*, not of proving by argument—that man is to be viewed in relation to the problem of being in general—in, that is, its most universal form—and that consequently man as man is unintelligible except and in so far as he himself is part of it. Indeed, properly speaking, he is the *locus* of the problem of being, the concrete reality in which being becomes problematic. The other concrete realities in our experience—animals, "things" in general—are as it were wholly sunk in being and present no problem. Man alone, as a being within the world, seeks to understand that larger *being* which includes him. At the same time, however, he perceives that the meaning of *his* being depends on the meaning of being-in-general, which itself remains to be decided, since it is the object of the metaphysical problem; which amounts to saying that man cannot understand himself, as the existent who actually raises the problem of being, unless and until he finds an answer to that question. In other words, anthropology (regarded as comprising not only psychology but all the humane sciences) depends as a whole on ontology, or the science of being *qua* being; or as Heidegger puts it, "Metaphysics belongs to the nature of a man", man's significance being essentially metaphysical.[1]

These are not merely idle speculations but facts of universal experience which it is the philosopher's task to do his best to elucidate. Such considerations, however, are not sufficient to afford us an adequate solution of the problem of the possibility of metaphysics as the science of being and its ultimate conditions. We have still to establish, as against every attempt at minimization, that this "ontological experience" is not an illusion in either content or form. All the same, we should be able to view and describe it as it presents itself, even whilst allowing that criticism must needs come later.

---

[1] *Was ist Metaphysik?* (Frankfurt-am-Main, 1949) p. 11. Heidegger's later works, especially "Überwindung der Metaphysik", in *Aufsätze und Vorträge* (1954), and above all *Zur Seinsfrage* (On the Question of Being) (1956), seem to tend in a rather different direction.

METAPHYSICS AND EXPERIENCE

Let us try, then, to see the elements of the problem as clearly as possible. The first point to note is that metaphysics is an investigation which begins with our primary experience of the world and ourselves and which is concerned with that experience as such. It is an experience far more general than that with which psychology or the positive sciences deal, all of which have determinate objects of study. For the question here is not of this or that experience in particular but concerns *the fact that there is an experience at all*. Hence we say that metaphysics' point of departure is the basic and universal experience that there is something, or that something *exists*. Experience in itself raises the problem of being —of being, that is, as we deal with it in its empirical concreteness; or in other words, as *something* which *is* (including both "essence" and "existence").

In a sense metaphysics never leaves the realm of experience. If the idea, which Henri Bergson was so fond of, of an "empirical metaphysics" is a somewhat ambiguous one, it nevertheless embodies a quantum of truth in so far as it signifies that metaphysics is rooted in ordinary concrete reality and even, in a way, never departs from it, thus meriting the designation "integral experience".[2] "I have made of metaphysics", Bergson wrote, "nothing but metaphysics, and yet I believe that my efforts could be described as a deepening of experience." Nothing indeed is more certain. Metaphysics is not, as is often supposed,[3] mere vague meandering of the mind, a cloud-land of airy notions, an old-fashioned and bemusing game; nor is it an excursion into unheard-of speculative systems. It is simply a reflection on experience itself as presented at once in its most concrete and comprehensive form with a view to grasping all its implications and intelligible demands. We shall see later on how, contrary to what

[2] H. Bergson, *La Pensée et le Mouvant*, p. 255.
[3] Thus did Aristophanes, in *The Clouds*, mock at Socrates.

is usually believed, it is the sciences of nature, not meta-physics, which are the truly abstract ones.

It is therefore a poor sort of metaphysics which would hasten to throw phenomena overboard, get rid of the visible and tangible, or else, it amounts to the same thing, confine itself to the mere technique or mechanism of thought. Nietzsche was much concerned to eliminate an "immaculate knowledge" to which (as his gibe went) none but utopia-mongers and star-gazers are ever drawn. Appearance, phenomena, the world of the senses constitute the road to meta-physics; or rather—for the metaphor of a *road* presupposes a continuity which does not exist—what really is implied is a *jump*; they provide the platform from which we start on our intellectual flight. Again, we may take them as *ciphers*, to use Karl Jasper's expression, which as such require interpreta-tion.[4] Appearance is appearance of being; the visible is the invisible manifested. That is why there can be no question of seeking the occult in what is visible and tangible: being, strictly speaking, is not hidden, since it is apparent to sense; nor is it "within", since it may be seen; nor yet is it "outside", because being cannot be external to anything. It is spoken of as "invisible" simply in order to signify that it is not visible as a *thing* and that it is offered only to the perception of the mind. And if we should happen to say that being is "in" the phenomenon it is because the unfortunate necessities of con-troversy betray us into using the quite inadequate language of empiricism and Kantianism. Actually, the phenomenon is the outward showing of being—in the proper sense of the word, its "manifestation"; and being is the meaning, the truth, of the phenomenon, of the thing seen.

TRANSCENDENCE

All this, let us repeat, is in no way intended to prejudge the solution to be offered to the problem of metaphysics, but

[4] *Philosophie* (Berlin, 1932), III, p. 121 f.

only to pose that problem correctly and in the terms which history, interpreting the spontaneity of reason, has always conceived of it. From this point of view we must admit, with Merleau-Ponty, that "a metaphysic begins from the moment when, ceasing to live solely by the evidence of the object as presented to the senses, or the object of science, we perceive the subjectivity . . . of all our experience, and, indissolubly bound up with this, its truth-value".[5] For if metaphysics is possible only on the basis of experience it is evident, on the one hand, that experience goes beyond that of the "object as presented to the senses" and is, properly speaking, experience of being in general and hence is the object, rather, of reason; and, on the other, that this "object" of reason can, from its very definition, be known only by reason—subjectively and reflexively, that is. But this is really to say that being, which is objective—in a sense, indeed, it is objectivity itself—is not, as such, an object; it is not a *thing*.

The point is one of prime importance. Fail to grasp it and metaphysics at once becomes something impossible and meaningless. This is the mistake into which empiricist doctrines (so-called) invariably fall: namely, of posing the question as though it were one simply of the existence or otherwise of objects or *things* that are non-sensible. Locke and Hume, for example, can never get away from presenting the metaphysical problem in these over-simplified terms, and many positivists (not to mention materialists) have followed suit without the least misgiving. To this we shall have to return later; but at our present stage we must state clearly that as envisaged by empiricists the metaphysical problem is unintelligible, for metaphysics has no greater foe than the worship of things. On the one hand it would be as self-contradictory to speak of "metaphysical objects" as of a "squared circle", since by definition every (particular) object is "physical". The difficulty would be lessened if we spoke of "metaphysical realities", on the hypothesis of a "world beyond

[5] *Sens et Non-sens* (Paris, 1948), p. 187.

sense"—itself calling for precise definition—to be apprehended, never as merely so many objects (or things), but as a *requirement of the understanding*, or a *necessary and absolute condition*. From this standpoint the "beyond-sense" would be more exactly described as *immanent in* sense-objects themselves, which alone are the immediate objects of our knowledge. It would be so, that is, as their *meaning* or *reason*, and as such no longer accessible to the organs of perception but only to mind working on sense-experience in order to render it intelligible. This was the traditional idea of metaphysics, an idea which the empiricists and Kant, as well as a good many moderns, have so little understood that in the end they have been content to ignore it, replacing it by a conception so inexact and inadequate as to amount to an *a priori* denial of the possibility of metaphysics at all.

It behoves us now, therefore, to give a more precise meaning to the term "beyond" as a description of the metaphysical or transphysical. To begin with it signifies that the metaphysical is at once immanent in sense-experience and yet transcends it. Like Bergson, we may well speak of it as a "deepening of experience". But "deepening" still carries with it a spatial suggestion, for however far or deeply one digs one still remains "in" the object or thing itself. The natural sciences, with all the vast resources at their disposal, are intent upon "deepening" man's experience, but they never break through the world of sense as such. "Transcending" would be a better word, did it not seem to imply a movement *outside* experience; whereas in fact we remain *within* experience, which involves both the senses and the reason, in order to apprehend its meaning and ground. But a thing's meaning is at once *immanent in* it—in so far as it is the truth about it— and *transcendent of* it—in so far as it can only exist in thought, idea or intuition. Metaphysics, as Plato would say, is certainly "over there", but this "over there" is also a "here".

However, this is not another way of saying that one may hope to reach the metaphysical either by enlarging and extending the empirical to infinity, or else by discovery of the infinitesimal or, as the pre-Socratic philosophers had begun by supposing, of an absolutely primary *element*. In reality, neither a quantitative "infinite" nor a primary element, if such indeed exist and can be displayed, is truly "over there" or "beyond": they are both radically and exclusively "here" and "now". No amount of matter, however great, and no element, however rarefied, can have a *meaning* only in and of themselves. Press the empirical as far as you will and you still will not wring this meaning from it, for it is something of a wholly different order from mere size. Extend it as far as you can and you still will not reach the metaphysical, however long your journey, unless you first cross a frontier. That is why we spoke just now of a "jump". Sheer immensity may perhaps discourage our attempts at measurement, but is not beyond measurement. The stars are many millions of light-years away from the earth, but yet are quite "near", almost within grasp! An "infinite" size is still absurdly small. There is no empirical "beyond"; at all events, the metempirical* is only relatively "beyond"; it is not the absolute beyond of metaphysics. Although science, in its more speculative aspect, can certainly mystify us, it cannot teach us anything that is of really vital concern to us as metaphysical animals, since it is entirely wrapped up in the "here-and-now". The "beyond" escapes it.

SENSE AND REASON

All the same, there is no concealing both the difficulty and the paradox of a science or mode of knowledge which, like metaphysics, is at once grounded in experience and yet claims to transcend it. Indeed, from the standpoint of positivism the paradox is irresolvable and the whole enterprise meaningless. But there are less sweeping objections, of which Merleau-Ponty, as we already have had occasion to notice, provides us with a clear general statement. Metaphysics consists, he says, in an attempt to grasp, at the same time and as bound up with one another, both "the radical subjectivity of our whole experience and its truth-value". That our experience is our own implies, on the one hand, "that it is not the measure of every imaginable thing in itself", and, on the other, "that it is nevertheless coextensive with every being of which we can form an idea". Thus, one can speak here of a metaphysical phenomenon, or, as Merleau-Ponty puts it, "a fundamental metaphysical fact", justifying the twofold assertion: "I am certain that being exists, so long as no other kind of being is meant than being-as-it-is-for-me." Let us try, then, to elucidate the content of these propositions. However clear they are in statement a good deal more is implied by them which should first be made explicit. What we need to do is less to contest them than to re-examine them critically, a task in which we may at once show the measure of truth they contain and yet go beyond them. Indeed to go beyond them is to bring out their truth.

To take these expressions at their face-value would, of course, obviate any need for discussing them, for they say nothing which one could not approve. Their difficulty lies, rather, in their leading to certain consequences which, in strict logic, do not follow. It must be admitted, to start with, that metaphysics begins with a refusal to "live in the evidence of the object", whether of ordinary sense-experience or of science. And this is just what we have already shown. But refusal of "the evidence of the object" here takes on a new meaning, which we have to consider. Husserl has carefully marked out the limits and dangers of this "psychologism of the evidence", which is at the root of all common-sense philosophies and which in fact is no more than a feeling differing from individual to individual and even in the same individual from moment to moment, according to the changing circumstances of his situation. In reality, the object, as such, is always open to question, and the fact that it is so constitutes the traditional form of metaphysics as "universal doubt"; for metaphysics as a science begins with that "fundamental crisis" in which the solid prestige of "objective" evidence is justly shaken. It could even be said without paradox that it survives only as a result of such questioning and that were it to give it up it would perish. "Evidence" can also impose an unconscious servitude, and it has been well remarked that the prisoners in Plato's famous allegory of the Cave were, in the first place, the prisoners of evidence.[6] If there is any matter on which the entire philosophical tradition is unanimous it is surely this. That is why critical doubt always accompanies inquiry. Coextensive with the whole of metaphysics, it proclaims this one essential purpose and continues to strive for an "evidence" acceptable only if it can be transformed and can show its credentials. Otherwise the prisoners in the cave would stay for ever the prisoners of evidence.

In a way, indeed, there is no evidence of the "object"; or if there is any, it is for reason alone, faced with an "object" grasped inwardly in the mind, in all the multiplicity of its relations, both internal and external, and in its primary meaning. It is of the nature of metaphysics that it should reach beyond the object as such to this meaning. It could also be fairly said that for metaphysics not only is there no "evidence" of the "object" but that there is really no such thing as an "object". Neither being nor God are "objects". Being— to risk speaking about it analogically—is not a "thing" but the immanent meaning of everything which in some manner or other exists; while God is even less an "object", since he is the principle of universal being and at once his own meaning and ground.

From yet another point of view it must be said that meta-

---

[6] J. Lagneau, *Célèbres leçons* (Paris, 1950), p. 32. Cf. Plato, *Republic*, VII, 1–2 (514 A, 517 B). In this famous allegory Plato compares the human soul in its present state—namely, in union with a body— to a prisoner chained in a cave with his back to the light. The prisoner cannot see the people and things passing by outside the cave's mouth in broad daylight, but only the shadows they throw up on its inner wall.

physics by mere definition excludes the evidence of the object, in so far as it transcends the object whether regarded as a datum of sense or as a thing. "Transcending" here connotes, in accordance with the meaning which contemporary phenomenology gives to the term, a "going beyond", or, more precisely and avoiding ambiguity, a *going-towards*. In the present instance it signifies "going towards" the meaning which is at once "in" what is apprehended by the senses and "beyond" it. For this in truth is how we should understand the term "metaphysics", both as a natural and spontaneous impulse of the mind and in its more developed and systematic forms.

Without, however, saying anything that might suggest begging the question we must try to give a rather more exact meaning to the "meta" in metaphysics, which itself implies transcendence of the object and a certain doubt about its "evidence". It often is badly enough explained, and objections are easily brought against it on that account. It goes without saying that, from one point of view, there is nothing beyond the object that signifies *for me*, at any rate if I expect to discover some other object such as would exist, not in any way for *me* but only and exclusively *in and for itself*. Actually, this "beyond" is not an "over there", but rather a "within", though a "within" that carries with it no spatial connotation. We have already noted the ambiguity here; but we have to use words as best we can and it is in fact impossible to do so without spatial metaphors. The important thing is not to be deceived by them and to realize at once that "within" simply means that the expression "beyond" indicates meaning or signification, and not a thing to be (as it were) unwrapped, as a kind of nucleus, and that in itself it is to be apprehended only by the mind. Not enough importance is attached to the familiar Thomist doctrine according to which God, if he exists, can be found only *through* the world, natural theology being an integral part of ontology or the science of being. Gabriel Marcel, who—with good reason—has never been slow to protest against notions that would turn God into an object, comparable, if you like, to a star vastly distant, no doubt, but detectable, potentially at least, by the telescope, does not see how God, as the Thomist tradition presents him, is any less an "object" than he is in his Cartesian setting. For there is no object—no particular object, that is—other than what is sensible. A mental object is such only as existing for thought, not as a "thing"; and its objectivity is that of "meaning" or "ground". In point of fact, there is only one object, the world itself; and metaphysics is through and through a science or knowledge of the world. What it envisages is less the chimerical and self-contradictory extra-mundane "reality" which the uncritical critic is apt to pose, than the *actual meaning of the world*, beyond all the objective evidences which, so far from providing the foundation of metaphysics, are an irremovable obstacle to it.

We shall admit, then, that "the metaphysical consciousness has no other objects than those of ordinary experience—the world around us, other people, human history, truth, culture",[7] seen not as bare facts—as *mere* "objects", that is—but as *significances*, constantly rediscovered in their basic novelty and through the sheer miracle of their occurrence. More briefly, it could be said that the sole object of all metaphysical reflection is man himself in his consciousness and his behaviour. For all cultural activities—art, science, religion—all social institutions, all history, are no more than the infinitely varying aspects in and by which man seeks, expresses and realizes himself within his universe. The science of being is above all the science of man who thinks universal being and thinks himself in the act of thinking being.

SUBJECTIVITY AND OBJECTIVITY

Is the necessary conclusion from all this, which, after all, is commonplace enough, that "we perceive the indissoluble

[7] M. Merleau-Ponty, *op. cit.*, p. 188.

connection between the radical subjectivity of our whole experience and its truth-value"? Yes and no. For it can be understood in more than one sense, each as it were overlapping the other, even though M. Merleau-Ponty does not tell us so explicitly.

Clearly there is no reason to question the "radical subjectivity of our whole experience" so long as it is only a matter of affirming that "our experience is our own". It could as easily be admitted that the "truth-value" of our experience is a function of that "radical subjectivity". The one quite certainly entails the other. We must be more precise, however. For what actually does the proposition mean, that "our experience is our own"? It implies, on the one hand, "that it is not the measure of every imaginable thing in itself", and, on the other, that "it is nevertheless coextensive with every being of which we can form an idea". It seems that we must understand that our experience is one-sided and limited, alike in its extent and in its modes, and that it cannot genuinely be considered to cover the totality of being. This is certain. Certain, too, is the fact—as well as no less evident—that every being of which we can form an idea—since it necessarily, as such, lies within the field of our experience, immediate or mediate—depends on the actual conditions of that experience. So much is obvious and raises no difficulty.

All the same, granting that our experience does not cover the totality of being, granting also that the primary meaning of "I think" is to afford us complete assurance (by that "experience of truth" to which Husserl justly appeals) that "being exists", why exactly should we be so reserved when it comes to locating the "basic metaphysical fact", explaining that this is possible only "on condition of one's not looking for any other sort of being than being-as-it-is-for-me"? It is a point which must be cleared up, since this "condition" admits of two different interpretations, between which it is of the utmost importance to distinguish.

On the one hand, indeed, we state it as absolutely certain

that no other kind of being is to be looked for than "being-as-it-is-for-me", because no other is possible. A being of any sort which did not exist for me would *ex hypothesi* lie wholly outside my experience and have no place in my knowledge. From this standpoint God, if he exists, is necessarily "for-me". In some manner or other he enters the field of my experience and thus necessarily assumes its form. But on the other hand it cannot be said, without going far beyond the evidence, that "being-for-me" is *only* for me. "If", writes Sartre, "we are all conscious of something then this 'something' must originally have had a *real* existence; one, that is, which is not simply relative to my consciousness."[8] M. Merleau-Ponty, however, seems both to avoid this paralogism, in emphasizing that "our experience is not the measure of every being imaginable in itself", and yet to imply it in his statement about the "radical subjectivity of our experience". We have already drawn attention to one perfectly acceptable and, in fact, obvious sense of these words. But for M. Merleau-Ponty there is another: namely, that being and truth refer to the strictly subjective aspect of our experience; although this experience is evidently to be taken as remaining fully "objective" *in the Kantian sense*.[9] This involves an assumption which not only is not justified by the premises relating to the conditions of knowledge, but is itself in conflict with the evidence— recognized nevertheless—that "being-for-me" is the form under which I apprehend "being-as-it-is-in-itself"—whatever the sense in which one may wish to understand such "being-in-itself". If not, the "paradox of consciousness and truth"[10] becomes even more "scandalous" than M. Merleau-Ponty supposes, since if it does not abolish the evidence that "being exists" it admits no more than the bare evidence of a world reduced to the pure subjectivity of a unique and isolated self.

[8] *L'Être et le Néant*, p. 588.
[9] We shall have to examine the Kantian idea of objectivity later (*infra*, pp. 54 f).
[10] Merleau-Ponty, *Sens et Non-Sens*, p. 187.

We shall not, then, look for any other kind of being than one which is "being-for-me". To do so would be absurd. But being-for-me is, in the first instance, *being*, and the whole task of metaphysics is to determine as exactly as possible what is the nature, structure and grounds of the being which my experience implies. For if it is certain, as we have already said in other words, that being, and the relatively stable structure which defines it, is not given as an absolute freed from the hazards of analysis—something which can be contemplated like an Idea in a heaven of intelligible realities (and this it is which makes our knowledge in a sense relative)— it is nevertheless beyond doubt that our experience, on pain of declining into the mere enumeration one by one of characteristics which have only an accidental connection symbolized by "and" and "also", is able to grasp in phenomena themselves and in their structures that which exactly constitutes their meaning and, in truth, their being, expressed in a concept which is, we may admit, perfectible and reformable but which does correspond to something that I actually meet with and that also transcends me. This surely is enough to remove the essential relativism with which M. Merleau-Ponty is clearly threatened.

A closer fidelity to the implications of an intentionality disentangled from these postulates—which unquestionably are idealist ones—would no doubt get rid of a relativism whose immediate result is to put both being and affirmation into perpetual disequilibrium. For the fundamental and determinative intentionality of our awareness is a dynamism whose exercise, nourished by a reflection which brings us back to the power or formal *a priori* which presides over it, reveals to us the mind's intrinsic openness to being in its totality. From this point of view the idea of being appears as regulating the whole activity of intentional consciousness; and in such a way that, by its universal and pervasive mediation—for here we have the very meaning of intentionality— ontology and phenomenology, as corresponding to the complex unity of phenomena and being, are reconciled and brought together in the unity of a single act of comprehension.[11]

But it must for that reason be said that "metaphysics begins with metaphysics".[12] From object to meaning there is no way but by a *qualitative* jump. As we pointed out at the beginning, the question of being is already in itself a wholly and inherently metaphysical one. Nothing is anterior to it, except that experience of being of which we have spoken and which really is one with it. This it is which Paul Ricœur so clearly shows in a passage where what he says of philosophy in general applies above all and unconditionally to metaphysics, which (to quote his words) "claims to be primary as a support or, rather, foundation", but which "cannot be so except on condition of being secondary from the standpoint of the source, the existential revitalizing, the original upsurge of energy". If metaphysics must have its presuppositions, it is its duty to examine them and then reabsorb them critically "into its proper starting-point". For "whatever has, to begin with, no *sources* has, thereafter, no autonomy."[13]

SPIRITUALISM AND MATERIALISM IN FACE OF EXPERIENCE

To the fundamental question of being two answers are theoretically possible; and both, in the course of time, have been given. They can be summed up in the words "materialism" and "spiritualism".

Materialism is based on the evidence of the senses as such. It admits, that is, as real and objective only what is tangible and measurable. All else is dream-thinking. Socrates, in Plato's *Theaetetus*, speaks of "those impious persons who

[11] Cf. Stanislas Breton: "Being and knowing address one another in a reciprocal intentionality, wherein they are mutually illumined" (*Conscience et Intentionalité* (Paris, 1956), p. 205).

[12] See V. Jankelevitch, *Philosophie première*. Introduction à la philosophie du "presque" (Paris, 1956).

[13] "Aux frontières de la philosophie," *Esprit*, November, 1952, pp. 755 and 760.

consider that nothing exists but what they can take hold of and press between their two hands, and who count as real nothing which is not visible".[14] Theaetetus thinks them hard and stubborn. But Socrates, perhaps, judges more perceptively in remarking that they are men who are "wholly strangers to the Muses", since, in fact, metaphysics and poetry are sisters. To this point we shall return. It is enough to state here that materialism has assumed many different forms, of which the commonest and most widespread in our day is what Auguste Comte, its most celebrated exponent, called *positivism*. *Scientism*, which relies only on the data of the positive or natural sciences, is but one variety of positivism. The same is true of *Marxism*, which propounds a "dialectical materialism". Materialism of any kind regards metaphysics, therefore, as an illusion. But if this is so it behoves it to offer an intelligible explanation of how the illusion grew up and how it has survived every attempt to get rid of it.

Spiritualism invokes the witness of consciousness. It claims that there is a world which the senses do not reach but which is in some way accessible to mind. This mind-world has at least as much reality as that which exists for the senses and for science, since the latter, far from being, as materialism asserts, the sole real world, is in the long run no more than appearance. Its being and coherence are the work of mind.

Thus we have two broad tendencies. For one of them being is simply the object of sense, and consciousness is but a reflection of the world of things. For the other it is mind, and the world of sense is no more than a mass of phenomena which derive such cohesion, permanence and intelligibility as they have from mind exclusively. How are we to reconcile them? Not by some *a priori* argument. On the contrary, it is clear that we must start with experience—but an experience which is both complete and duly analysed into its data and its implications. This presupposes a careful definition of the conditions of that experience.

[14] 155 E.

The first thing to note is that it is not so much the experience itself which is in question as the meaning and basis of it. That experience of being is a fact—however understood—materialism and spiritualism are agreed. *Something* exists. The problem is to explain what this "something" is. Now the very experience of "something" seems to indicate that the "something existing" is to be identified with *contingency,** since the being of which we have experience, and in the first instance the being that I am, is a matter of becoming: it is born and it dies; and it is incessantly turning into something else, thus proving that it would be capable of *not* being—in other words, that it is not necessary. Experience is therefore, properly speaking, an *experience of contingency*.

Now this experience, as such, is in itself a metaphysical experience, even the basic metaphysical experience. For becoming, in its empirical elements—however complex these may be, and however amazingly elusive—raises only the sort of empirical problems which in theory science can answer, the actual limits of the positive sciences here being a question of fact and not of principle. But the fact of becoming, in its totality, is a mystery, since I who form part of this process, and who at every moment am swept along and away with it, can still detach myself from it *in thought*. Face to face both with the eternity which every instant of time embodies—to that extent each instant is, as it were, a denial of time —and with the flight of all such instants, since each must die in order to live again, I am puzzled by the strangeness of a destiny for which death is at once a necessity and a scandal. A congenital weakness, a relentless mortality, permeate a being which in itself transcends death. I who am in process of being can in thought abolish the very thing—process, becoming—which defines me.

Thus it follows that the basic experience is at the same time an *experience of finitude*. Everywhere man encounters limits: in things, the being of which is precarious and ever-changing and which serve his ends only at the price of an exhausting effort; in his thought, which runs up against the unknown and incomprehensible and is ever subject to error; in his life, always subject to suffering and death; in his conscience, which struggles with and so often yields to the powers of evil. The sense of this irremediable finitude is expressed in a *refusal* of experience as it actually comes to us—in a profound conviction, that is, of its radical insufficiency. As such, the experience of finitude itself includes an *experience of reason and conscience*, which are, so to speak, the positive or correlative aspect of this negative one. By the same impulsion, as we have observed, man becomes aware both of his limitations and also of something within him which protests against these limitations, trying to overcome them and so transcend all determination.* It is, in fact, in the experience of contingency that the whole human drama is rooted.

Every metaphysic, even a negative one like materialism, must, accordingly, have its beginning in this experience, which is the final summing-up of all that, at the outset, we subsumed under the designation "metaphysical phenomenon". But for the time being we must confine ourselves to these general considerations. The study of metaphysics as a science, in its content and its problems, will have to take up the question again from a more positive angle.

CHAPTER III

IS THERE AN ABSOLUTE?

THE DEMAND FOR AN ABSOLUTE

Several consequences follow from what we have just been saying, and should be noted. The first is that the answer to the question of being must be an *absolute* answer; it must, that is to say, offer a complete justification of our primary experience. This implies preception of the contingent's correlate: namely, the absolute, throughout the triple realm of being, thought and value (or action). In saying that, however, we have no wish to prejudge anything, since what fundamentally we are concerned with now is a question of method. But the requirements of the method are rigorous: short of a refusal to give one at all (which would seem to be impossible) every reply, if it amounts to anything, must posit an absolute, for the absolute alone answers for all the rest; while if at the same time it is the perfect Absolute, beyond all relativity, it answers for itself. From this point of view materialism would tell us that everything is explicable in terms of matter; spiritualism, on the contrary, that everything is explicable in terms of mind. It is for either answer to justify itself in respect of the totality of our experience.

It has to be observed, nevertheless, that the very principle which makes the absolute of being and of the several orders of being a rigorous and necessary methical (and logical) demand has itself been called in question. Thus, according to a contemporary writer, G. Gusdorf, in his recent *Treatise on Metaphysics:* "Renunciation of the absolute makes possible a metaphysic of man. Indeed, every incarnation of the absolute penalizes human existence, which forthwith appears relative and fallen."[1] Here, of course, we recognize the Sartrean theme. Merleau-Ponty, for his part, would certainly endorse it. We shall find the same difficulty when we come to discuss value. Here it is the problem of metaphysics which is in question, where an objection of Merleau-Ponty's has the advantage of putting the issue with great clarity.[2] "The metaphysical consciousness", he writes, "dies when in contact with the absolute because it is itself, beyond the 'flat' world of a merely conventional or sleeping consciousness, the vital link between me and myself and between myself and other people."[3]

The more general sense of this objection is that the absolute, whether of thought or of value, inevitably produces the kind of conventionalism or mental sleep which is the death of consciousness and conscience (above all when it induces a "good" conscience), both because it smothers anxiety and nourishes a self-assured complacency and because it eliminates what is capable of being tested and proved true—which necessarily presupposes an experience which is progressive and always open to revision—in favour of a "truth" which, deemed to be final and complete, prevents from the outset any real movement of the mind. So be it, let us say. But at this level, and under a form no less general, is it not obvious that all such argumentation applies equally well to him who advances it? For rejection of the absolute, whether of thought or of value, becomes itself, in Merleau-Ponty's own context, a "truth" both final and complete,

[1] *Traité de Métaphysique* (Paris, 1956), p. 167.

[2] The word "Absolute", according to Lalande's *Vocabulaire technique et critique de la philosophie*, found its way into technical philosophical usage only at the beginning of the nineteenth century, with Maine de Biran and Victor Cousin. We have already quoted a passage in which Descartes states it as a rule of method to look for what in all things is most nearly *absolute*. It is more, however, than a matter of words. The search for the absolute (under whatever name) is a universal fact. On this Lalande agrees.

[3] *Sens et Non-Sens*, p. 191.

preventing any future progress of the mind. Thus we are confronted with yet another absolute!

However, let us pass this over and try to get to the root of the problem. We shall have no difficulty in admitting that the "absolute", as Merleau-Ponty seems to conceive it, would in effect be the death of thought and the end of morality. We are not concerned with a certain arrogant, categorical and aggressive way of (so to speak) *taking charge* of the absolute, of talking, legislating and condemning in its name, which clearly is the death of all metaphysical consciousness as of all spirit of inquiry and capacity for free dialogue. Let us leave such self-assured "absolutists" to their dogmatism. If there are any "pilgrims of the absolute" they should know that the journey is long and arduous, that side-tracks abound and mirages are frequent. But what here is in dispute goes much further, since it bears, not on some questionable procedure merely, but on the absolute itself. Indeed, the absolute, in some way present in all thought and in every moral valuation, is reduced simply to "my experience of harmony with myself and with other people"; or at least this experience alone, it is said, can give meaning, in so far as it has any substance at all, to "my belief in the absolute". Unhappily, the absolute as thus understood would be of no use, since "whether or not there is an absolute thought and, in regard to practical problems, an absolute valuation, I am in a position to judge only my own opinions, which remain liable to error, however closely I scrutinize them".[4]

This kind of argument clearly depends on the same implicit assumptions as we noted above in regard to the problem of the meaning of metaphysics, which consisted in supposing that an absolute of being, if such exist, would be of no significance, since there can never be any other sort of being than "being-as-it-is-for-me". In each case the answer must be the same. In fact, just as there is, in "being-as-it-is-for-me", an absolute of being, and as also my experience

<hr>

[4] Merleau-Ponty, *op. cit.*, pp. 189 and 190.

embodies an objectivity which controls it, so too all thought and all morality imply an absolute alike of truth and of value. But if being cannot be given apart from "being-as-it-is-for-me", even more certainly the absolutes of thought and of value cannot be apprehended apart from living and concrete thought and moral activity. And as our science of being derives from our experience, which is inexhaustible, so also the absolute of either thought or morality is revealed and gradually elaborated in the continuous experience which we, along with the whole human race, have of the life of the mind and of moral action. That is why nothing prevents us saying that "my belief in the absolute, in so far as it has any substance, is only my experience of a harmony with myself and other people", provided we understand—if at least we wish to avoid the postulate of a "radical subjectivity"—that this harmony of myself with myself is that of the empirical, diurnal self with one in which the demand for the absolute and universal is insistent, and by which harmony with others becomes at the same time both possible and necessary. Such precisely is the central theme of the philosophies of Lachelier and Lagneau; moreover, it links up with the authentic traditions of Western intellectualism. Otherwise, what would this self-harmony mean but a sterile identity or a pointless tautology?

Yet the absolute, it will be said, even in this doctrinal context, would prove to be of little use, since in all respects it would have to come down, so to speak, into the contingent world of discourse; while the self, with its supposedly immanent absolute, would be obliged to join in dialogue with others and thus share the doubts and uncertainties which are always present at the empirical level. I can never judge and evaluate except by way of my own opinions, and there is no guarantee whatever that they will not finally turn out to be wrong. This is really the most direct and comprehensive objection to the idea of an absolute, and hence to all metaphysics as traditionally understood. But it seems to rest on a misconception, precisely in so far as it consists in depicting the absolute as in some manner external to thought, both theoretical and practical. An absolute of this kind, if one can conceive it intelligibly, would surely be the death of thought and morality alike. It would abolish all problems at a single stroke. In any case, it would be sufficient, as Bergson says, to consult "the master's book" to have infallible knowledge of what one ought both to think and do. But the truth is, rather, that an absolute of this sort is no more than a myth. God no doubt is indeed the Absolute of thought and of value, and all good and all truth are to be defined in relation to him. But it is no less certain that our relation with the divine Absolute is a matter of actual experience and that it is in and by our own activity, gradual and laborious as it is, that we "realize" it, though without ever being able to say that this "realization" is complete. If there be an absolute of thought and value it still does not save us from thinking only with difficulty or evaluating precariously. In the same way that the absolute of being is, as we have seen, always immanent in "being-as-it-is-for-me", so the absolute of thought inheres in thought as the immanent principle of its activity; it is the actual experience of thought in all its infinitely varied historical forms, in its successes and its failures, which gradually enables us to become more fully and clearly aware of what there is in it that is absolute and universal. In the same way, too, it is mankind's constantly renewed effort, despite so many mistakes, failures and crimes, which makes us capable of attaining to a truer and deeper sense of morality. But neither in the intellectual order nor in that of our moral activity would this progress, tortuous and ever doubtful though it is, become possible, were there not an absolute of thought and value already present to thought and the moral consciousness, by virtue of a *demand* which, in fact, is its definition and which, as such, can only become explicit in the actual process of human history.

It is therefore true that "there is no absolute knowledge",[5] if by "absolute knowledge" is to be understood a rule or law or evidence external to knowledge itself, or if what is envisaged is a knowledge at once perfect, definitive and irreformable. It is because of this "gap", allowably, that "we are open to philosophy"; or, in other words, that philosophy is something not already complete but always to be completed. But because there is no "absolute knowledge" it does not follow that there is nothing absolute *in* knowledge, for there is at least that demand for the absolute which alone gives meaning to knowledge. Could the idea of "absolute knowledge" even be denied without at the same time implying an absolute? And how could the absence of this "absolute knowledge" be a "gap" without also being, under the form of that basic demand, simultaneously a presence?

RATIONAL DISCOURSE

A second consequence is that metaphysics always presents itself—however we may understand it and even when we deny it—as an undertaking essentially rational and critical, since it is a matter of interpreting experience and discovering its deeper meaning. The point is one which Plato is constantly stressing, especially in the *Phaedo*, where he declares that "things known by the senses evoke another reality than that of concrete beings", and that as a result "the true reality can be known only by means of rational thought".[6] If the term "positive" be taken in the same sense as it bears in the sciences—that is, as connoting an experience simply of *things* —there neither is nor can be any "positive" metaphysics. Metaphysics, by its very definition, is a search for meaning and grounds, for absolute meaning and grounds. Now the absolute, however we conceive it, is not a thing, but is itself the condition of things. Although implied in experience, it is accessible only to reason.

[5] M. Merleau-Ponty, *Éloge de la philosophie* (Paris, 1955) p. 55.
[6] 79 A.

That also is why, *in this sense*, there neither is nor can be an "experience of the absolute". In a work from which we have already quoted, Gusdorf goes to much trouble to argue this, and so leaves the whole question on one side. It is an omission, moreover, not without excuse, since very many modern thinkers consider themselves unable to meet the objections of positivism except by invoking an "experience" or "intuition" of the absolute such as we ourselves decline to admit without in any way feeling obliged to reject that "metaphysical experience" which we have been trying to describe and analyse. For "experience" is not a univocal* term: our experiences are not necessarily experiences of *things*; it could even be, as we have already shown in criticizing the idea of *object*, that experience of mere things—our human condition being what it is—is neither the clearest nor the most certain. Objectivity is not to be equated simply with the notion of an object.

At this point, however, we come up against the solid and deep-seated objections raised by Kant's criticism of "pure reason", which leads to a fundamental transformation of the whole idea of objectivity, to the extent of reducing it to what the philosophy of common sense calls, quite properly, the "subjective", thus turning metaphysics into a construction at once gratuitous and necessary, in so far as it is determined by the *a priori* forms of the understanding and sensibility. In fact, so Kant states, all objective knowledge is perforce contained within the limits of experience. Hence there is no legitimate use of the understanding except in relation to the data of sense-apprehension. Its one and only function is to determine phenomena and establish them as objects. Any attempt to transcend sense-experience is therefore impossible and a sophistry. The very fact that metaphysics purports to deal with transcendent realities—the "self", the world as a unity, God as the absolute, and, in general, all ultra-phenomenal being—renders it unjustifiable. The absolute, if there is one, must needs lie beyond the grasp of knowledge.

Kant no doubt recognized that the phenomenon, in consequence of what he call its "passive genesis"—from the fact that it is born in us and in its brute reality does not depend on us—is not and cannot be its own support and that it somehow calls for a reality beyond itself. But this "beyond", Kant tells us, is an unknowable. It is apprehended only negatively, as the unsurpassable limit of sense-experience. Being is transcendent, but *in itself* is unattainable.

This famous doctrine, the influence of which has left so profound a mark on modern speculative thought, would demand a lengthy discussion such as cannot be undertaken here. We shall note simply that the manner in which Kant poses the problem of metaphysics as a whole constitutes, in fact, a *petitio principii*. For the Kantian solution is already contained in the way the question is put, Kant having previously taken as his starting-point the empiricism of Hume. If he disowns this connection in order to account for metaphysical realities, substituting for it the *a priori forms** of sensibility and understanding, that doctrine's all-pervading empiricism is purely and simply a postulate amounting to an initial *a priori* denial that a meta-physical *science* is at all possible.

It is true that there is a "Kantian metaphysic": that which results from the action of the *a priori* categories of pure reason, described by Kant as "objective", in view of which he has no hesitation in saying that metaphysics is a science indispensable to human reason. But this "metaphysic", by virtue of its own structure, is in truth only a "logic"—or perhaps a "transcendental logic"*. The objectivity on which it prides itself is no more than the fact of its being the universal condition of the entire world of objects in their formal reality. All of which, strictly speaking, is sheer hypothesis. It is, however, in Kant's eyes, a dogmatic solution such as will not admit the validity of any other conception. Now it is easy to see that the Kantian dilemma (based on empiricism) between the "association of ideas" (or chance, as Kant himself remarks) and the *"a priori* forms" disregards—to the extent of not even envisaging it as a hypothesis—the solution (which might be described as intermediary) of an *intellectual intuition*. Kant states indeed, as if the assertion dispensed with proof, that "the concept *in no way* derives from experience" and that it is absolutely *a priori* inasmuch as an abstraction founded on sense cannot yield us concepts going beyond the sphere of sensible knowledge. For however far the abstraction may be pushed, the concepts, instead of becoming "intellectual" in the true sense of the word, persist as sensible concepts (i.e. images).[7]

The *petitio principii* is manifest; for the sole reason which Kant adduces in order to question the possibility of "intellectual intuition"—in other words, an apprehension of the intelligible, or of meaning, in the sensible itself—and therefore of metaphysics "in the real sense" (for Kant readmits it "in the formal sense"), and thus to justify that divorce between thought and being which is the theme of the *Critique*, is that an abstraction resting on sense can yield us nothing but what pertains to sense and is merely a generalization of the images with which sense-experience provides us. But that is precisely the point at issue. The division of judgments into *a priori* analytic* and synthetic*, the theories of the categories* of pure reason and the mechanism of the schemes of the understanding[8] are so many aspects of this initial and arbitrary assumption. The problem remains, therefore, unresolved. Even after Kant the question persists whether a science of metaphysics "in the real sense" is possible.

It should be observed, however, that our criticism of Kant bears much more upon his specific arguments than upon his fundamental position. For we must agree with him, on the

[7] Kant, *Dissertatio de mundi sensibilis atque intelligibilis forma et principiis* (1770).

[8] Kant's theory of the *schemes of the understanding* is aimed at reconciling (as it were) pure reason, i.e. the purely formal *a priori* categories, with sense—i.e. pure matter, without form—which Kantian doctrine otherwise appears wholly to separate. But the theory is only a device, as ineffective as it is complicated and obscure, for masking this separation.

one hand, that the absolute of reason and being cannot be a *thing* such as might conceivably be grasped and, so to say, isolated within the framework of experience—a point of cardinal importance on which we have had more than once to insist; and, on the other, that the Absolute *par excellence*— the sole Absolute—can in no way be brought within the bounds of the strictly definable. For the Absolute, being "given" in experience—which it conditions through and through—as an ultimate principle of intelligibility, is by definition beyond all particular determination,* even a purely intelligible one. Rather, as itself the source of all determinations, whether of thought or of being, it is the motivating impulse of our search, manifesting itself only as that "drive towards transcendence" of which Karl Jasper speaks.[9] Thinkers who, like Malebranche and Gioberti, have believed it possible to apprehend the absolute in what philosophers call indeterminate and infinite being, have failed to see that being as we know it in experience, even in its most generalized form, is still, because of its potential multiplicity, a determination, and that the absolute whence it proceeds would, in regard to such being, as St Thomas points out,[10] be Over-being rather than being. It remains, and this Kant failed to see, that the Absolute is self-affirmed in us by its actual presence and that this self-affirmation is known by what we have called *intellectual intuition,* which in fact is the power of transcending the limits alike of sense and reason.

Hence the evident difference between intellectualism and rationalism. The latter, typically Kantian, believes it possible to establish a *closed system* by purely rational means. From this standpoint either the absolute (or God) is identifiable with the world, rationalized by knowledge or the positive sciences; or else an "other-worldly" absolute is postulated non-rationally. But such ways as these of approaching the problem destroy the very idea of an absolute: the first in

[9] *Philosophie* (Berlin, 1932), III, pp. 4f.
[10] *De Veritate*, qu. 2, art. 1, ad 9.

relativizing it, since, as St Thomas has shown in his argument from the degrees of being, the multiple is a contradiction of the absolute, which, if it exists at all, cannot but be One; the second in objectifying it as an arbitrary and unthinkable *x*, utterly foreign to the world of experience, whereas the Absolute, if it exists, must itself be the principle and ground of experience as a whole. Intellectualism, on the contrary, in perceiving that mind is something beyond mere reasoning, sees within the rationally intelligible itself—within the world of knowledge, that is—a demand for the transcendent which from the very outset excludes any "closed system", in the conviction that all such systems are but the circumference which reason draws round itself, thus becoming a prisoner within its own periphery. So it harks back to an Absolute apart from which this power of transcending all systems, all concepts and all data would be wholly inconceivable. The Absolute is, then, at one and the same time presence and appeal, immanence and transcendence.

METAPHYSICS AND METAPHYSICAL SYSTEMS

A third consequence of the fact that every metaphysic can be described as a making explicit of the metaphysical phenomenon (or experience) and that it is self-originating—since man, to start with, is *metaphysical* before becoming a *metaphysician*—is that metaphysics does not begin with some *person*, even a great philosopher, but, strictly speaking, with nothing at all—or with everything. Contrary to what happens in the case of the natural sciences, which together form a whole to which every particular result makes a further contribution, so that the physicist, for example, sets out from certain partial but, so far as they go, assured results, metaphysics, being always and in all circumstances a questioning of everything (or, if you will, of the *sum* of things), cannot but begin with that "metaphysical experience" which is already all that metaphysics essentially is. "The question of

being", says Heidegger, "springs from a preconceptual understanding of being." Metaphysics is not, then, under any obligation to justify its beginnings; otherwise it would have to
precede itself. In fact, however, it exists so soon as there
occurs that intellectual intuition or apprehension of the absolute conditions of being which is intrinsically one with it.
Thus metaphysics is indefinitely anticipated in the power of
thought inherently directed towards the absolute and universal significance of experienced being. It originates, accordingly, in that "nothing" which is simply the mind as principle
of intelligibility: a "nothing", however, which also is "everything", since all metaphysical experience is in some way
comprised therein.

But we must not misconceive the rôle of the great metaphysicians in history. How could we, without arrogance, fail
to interrogate those whom we refer to as "key-thinkers"? In
a sense every metaphysic is a dialogue with the greatest minds
of history—Parmenides and Heraclitus, Plato and Aristotle,
Plotinus and St Augustine, St Thomas and Descartes, Kant
and Hegel, Comte and Marx; not to mention the thinkers of
the East, more concerned as they are with "wisdom" than
with speculative knowledge. Actually there is no isolated
metaphysic. We work, so to speak, as a team. Indeed, as Plato
suggested, "all thought is dialogue".[11] The metaphysical experience whence every philosophy draws its nourishment is
so vast, rich, complex and profound, that there cannot be
too many such systems—wherein, it may be, we shall see
nothing but denial and contradiction—in order to awaken us
to all the various aspects of the universe and of man. Even
the doubters and the sceptics bring their contribution. Without a certain basic accord the struggle itself would not have
been possible. Every metaphysic is a dialogue, an attempt at
communication impelled by the longing for communion.[12]

[11] *Sophist*, 263 C.
[12] Hence the advent of metaphysics, in its opposition to mere animal
instinct, is inherently a renunciation of violence. See Eric Weil,
Logique de la Philosophie (Paris, 1955), p. 2.

On the other hand, however, this dialogue, as St Augustine has so well shown in his *De Magistro*, is not and cannot be only a passive reception of the "master's" answers, especially as these answers are not always in agreement, either as between one philosopher and another or even in the same thinker, who, after all, has ceased neither to inquire nor to change. It cannot but serve to open our minds to ever deeper personal reflection, in helping us to penetrate more and more fully and clearly into the abundant variety and meaning of that metaphysical experience of which we all, great and small, learned or ignorant, are equally sharers. Already, in the sphere of concrete action, such experience provides the luminous spontaneity which seeks expression in conscious thought; it is the living thought presupposed by that reflective thought which at once articulates and justifies it, and which in the end enables the demand for the absolute implicit in human life to become manifest.[13]

Here indeed, as we said above, borrowing an idea of St Augustine's, the true interlocutor is that interior Master who expresses himself in and by means of our reason and who encourages us to remain always and to the end submissive to the demand for intelligibility which is at the root of all metaphysics. Hence it is said that in metaphysics nothing is prejudged, although there are accepted truths which nevertheless have to be retrieved, as it were, and reassimilated by means of that capacity for wonder which, as we have noted, is the primary condition of all metaphysics. What Alain says about culture, that "it does not transmit itself", and that "to be cultured must always mean, in any field, one's going back to the fount itself and drinking from the palm of one's own hand and not merely from a borrowed cup",[14] applies above all to metaphysics, which is *par excellence* the culture of the mind and in truth of the whole man. For in this we possess

[13] Such is the point of St Thomas' admirable discussion of "Whether one man can teach another" in the *Summa Theologica*, Ia, qu. 117, art. 1.

[14] *Propos sur l'éducation*, XLV, p. 172.

only what we have acquired and won by our own efforts, our own reflection. No mere repetition, however accurate, of the familiar text-book thesis will ever be proof of knowledge or of metaphysical aptitude. What is needed is a passion for truth more than for syllogisms.

It might also be said that, in a sense, metaphysics offers no "answer", if by answer is meant a solution which would dispense with all further reflection and obviate all necessity for re-examining the reasons for it or even for that initial wonder in which inquiry originates. The positive sciences, up to a certain point at least, can reach conclusions which render further question unnecessary. On the contrary, metaphysics is a continuous interrogation; its solutions are themselves problems and a challenge to a renewed quest. Far from bringing all inquiry to an end, it carries us on to still further questionings. Such answers as it is able to supply are acceptable only if they remain "open", as though nothing after all had been finally settled. The great metaphysicians themselves have not always realized this. Descartes, for example, supposed that a few hours' meditation in the course of a lifetime would be enough to solve all our metaphysical difficulties, coming at last to believe (and in fact to state) that his own philosophy would bring men's doubts on that score to an end. But in so doing he forgets how he himself started—namely, on the day when he "resolved to study myself also and to employ all the forces of my mind in choosing the road that I should take".[15] Pascal saw more clearly when he observed that the answers of philosophy have constantly to be made afresh, both in history and in personal reflection, unless we commit them to the memory—and that, he declares, is not reason but only custom and sleep.[16] Metaphysics, then, is not a sort of landed property the rentals of which are always at our disposal, a banking-account on which we are ever free to draw cheques. On the contrary, it is something wholly gratuitous and an endless

[15] *Discourse on Method*, conclusion of Part One.
[16] *Pensées* (ed. Brunschvicg), 369, 543.

need. Starting with that "nothing" which yet is "all things", the great metaphysicians bequeath to their successors and to such as go to them for wisdom nothing, to all intents, other than the obligation to carry on the pursuit—which means, in fact, beginning all over again.

METAPHYSICS AND POETRY

If this beginning really is—we must repeat the word—"nothing", yet neither is it mere zero. To set out from zero would be identical with never setting out at all. Nothing, in this context, is not "nothingness", vacuity. Far from that, it signifies an initial abundance—the paradox that the answer is always present in the question itself (since man would not seek the answer had he not already found it). In other words, we have, on the one hand, *experience as a whole*—called in question, however, by the sheer wonder which it provokes; and, on the other, *reason*—though a reason without bias and careful only to obey its own inherent dynamism: a dynamism revealed in intellectual intuition and expressed in the pre-reflective forms of the "metaphysical phenomenon" as something to be explained, clarified and criticized, but in no wise abolished.

It is certain, indeed—and it is this which the Kantian criticism has enabled us to see more clearly—that metaphysical achievement implies an idea of reason as the power of knowing and *conceiving* what the imagination cannot *represent*: the conviction that human rationality is capable of grasping, within experience itself, the principles which justify that experience in being what it is, and, in the first instance, in *being*, purely and simply. For metaphysics is, as such, the fact of a thought which in some way thinks what is universal and eternal, and which establishes relations that are necessary, ideal and consistently valid. Non-temporal and impersonal, it transcends entirely what is empirical—the content of sense-experience. Metaphysics is so closely linked therefore with what may be described as "rational optimism" that every doubt about the power and scope of the understanding immediately becomes a doubt about metaphysics as a science. This is certainly what Kant's work so clearly shows. In his perspective, the realm of the metaphysical, when not denied outright, becomes accessible only by way of an irrationalism —feeling, or faith, or tradition—as, among others, Joseph de Maistre and Lammennais have maintained. For such is the standpoint of all "fideists".

Must we, then, begin by establishing the value and scope of reason? Nearly all modern philosophy, since Descartes, has isolated this preliminary critical investigation under the name of "theory of knowledge". The very idea of it is not an altogether happy one, since a critique of reason must itself make use of reason. It is difficult to say *a priori* whether metaphysics is possible or not. The fact is that it exists, both in a spontaneous and "natural" form and in one that is learned and systematic—as a science, that is, properly so called. The latter comes into being as soon as a naïve awareness develops into a reflective. Man embarks on the metaphysical quest from the moment he distinguishes himself from the world around him, opposing himself to it in the name of selfhood and consciousness—in a word, from the moment he recognizes his own humanity. This quest may be undertaken without any concern to establish its legitimacy. As Louis Lavelle has said:

> Preliminary inquiries of this kind can only delay and embarrass reflective thought. To question the legitimacy of something which has not yet come into existence will inevitably lead to a negative answer. Here, as in everything else, there is no other method open to us than to push our thinking as far as it will go. What the results will be will soon become obvious, as also will the appropriateness of the word "metaphysics" to cover them. Here, as in everything else, the proof of the pudding is in the eating. You demonstrate the possibility of metaphysics in the actual process of doing it.[17]

[17] "Les Trois moments de la métaphysique", in *La philosophie française* (Paris, 1950), p. 132.

We cannot in this connection too often recall a profound remark of Fichte's who, on August 30th, 1795, wrote to Jacobi: "It was pride which first led us to philosophize, and because of it we have lost our innocence." Assuredly there is a way of presenting metaphysics as a science which simultaneously makes it practically impossible by throwing doubt, at the outset, on the very conditions of metaphysical thinking —on the experience realized in the "innocence" or spontaneity of a reason which acts according to its own dynamism. Pride—the boast of being absolutely self-sufficient, capable of rebuilding everything absolutely *de novo* and so turning oneself into God—has again and again marred the beginnings of philosophical thought. We may even allow that all philosophy, like everything human, has something impure in it and carries the burden of an original sin (delivery from which is possible only on entering the realm of grace). And if it is true that the proper task of metaphysics is to question all things by a method of universal doubt, such doubt itself can only be fruitful when exercised with humility and generosity, by the light of that inner illumination of which Malebranche so often speaks. Thanks to which, as Fichte says in the passage already quoted, we can "discover our nudity" and thereafter philosophize, not any longer out of pride, but "for our salvation". Doubt of this kind truly is, in Heidegger's phrase, "piety of thought".

Poetry certainly can teach the metaphysician something, for poetry has a greater simplicity and as a rule is closer to our ordinary experience. Aristotle tells us with complete confidence that poetry, of all literary media, is the most philosophic, and Descartes holds that there are "seeds of knowledge which are brought to light by the reason of the philosophers and by the imagination of the poets".[18] The same idea finds an echo, in our day, in Heidegger's belief that it is in the work of certain poets that the profoundest metaphysical truth is to be sought. Poetry, in fact, seeks to express or to

[18] *Cogitationes privatae* (ed. Adam and Tannery), X, p. 217.

suggest the ineffable—in a word, that metaphysic before metaphysics which is the source of every system (since apart from it they are mere castles of sand). It translates metaphysical experience, but into symbols and images; feels more than it reasons; sees rather than discourses. The logical mind may laugh at it, but in doing so it reveals its own poverty because, when confronted with the sheer mystery of life, man can after all only babble. The poet reveals to us what we cannot utter, coming as it does from the depths of the heart; for as Edgar Allan Poe says, the poet's visions, far richer and diviner than any scientific construction, enclose those "unthought-like thoughts that are the souls of thought".[19] Poe adds, it is true, that he has "the most sovereign contempt" for poet-metaphysicians—though with the qualification, "as poets". The truth is that poetry is metaphysical, not of set choice, but, as it were, unwittingly, by the mere fact of its profound and humble concern with an experience which it lives rather than contemplates.

Yet even if there is a metaphysical poetry worthy of the name of poetry it still is not metaphysics. In drawing us into the depths of the soul, in disclosing to us the inherent mystery of things, it does not perform the salutary and difficult task of self-criticism.[20] Its intuition is rich and full of charm, but the philosopher must needs translate it into language, into a coherent discourse, that is, dependent upon reason and logic. Lastly, it is the metaphysician who has to gather up the "revelations" of the poet and confront them with that metaphysical experience whence both alike derive. But it would be an abject failure on the philosopher's part were he to lose sight of the meaning of the poetry and become insensitive to the beauty of its song.

With this reservation, and because, in spite of all, reasoning

[19] *Works*, iii (Poems and Essays), p. 24.
[20] "The creations of poets," says Socrates (*Apology*, 22 C) "are to be attributed to divine inspiration. They utter many beautiful things, but they have no real understanding of what they express." Cf. *Ion*, 533 D f. and *Phaedrus*, 244 A f.

and argument are unavoidable, we shall try to construct a metaphysic. But there are several ways of doing so; and we shall select the one that best suits the preoccupations and interests of our own day, which has been so dazzled by the stupendous developments in natural science that it can scarcely conceive any other way of reaching authentic knowledge than that of the disciplines which it refers to as "positive". Not that we have ever supposed that metaphysics could establish itself as an extension of the sciences of nature. We have seen that it can begin only with a jump—in other words, only with itself; although this is not an *a priori* assumption but the very definition of what metaphysics is. Yet a kind of reasoning *ad absurdum* is by no means out of place here, by pushing to its logical conclusion the positivist argument according to which the natural sciences offer a sufficient account of the entire field of the knowable and affirmable, and by inquiring whether and how, on this hypothesis, a whole order of reality does not remain for ever outside that which the sciences explore and of which they provide, at their own level and by their appropriate methods, a presumably exhaustive knowledge. We then shall see, perhaps, how metaphysical science discloses a range of problems that are quite specifically its own and independent of all others. Finally, we shall have to attempt to answer the questions thus raised and to construct, as far as possible and by the appropriate methods (in the light of all our preceding observations), a science of metaphysics itself.

PART II

THE SCIENCE OF METAPHYSICS

CHAPTER IV

METAPHYSICS AND THE SCIENCES

THE PROBLEM

Certain facile attempts to get rid of metaphysics altogether may be disregarded. For the philosophers of the Enlightenment it was no more than a disease of thought. Hume sees in it merely a product of language; and Léon Brunschvicg, in much the same vein, can discover nothing other than a projection of the "ontological imagination". What we have said so far, however, provides, we believe, a sufficient answer to this sort of argument. Nevertheless the neo-positivists of the Vienna Circle have tried more recently to give such views a strictly cogent form. Their standpoint may be summarized thus: All metaphysical assertions are and can only be *nonsense*, inasmuch as metaphysics purports to describe a reality that lies beyond experience; but what cannot be verified—i.e. that for which no possible verification could be adduced—is not a proposition. The basic postulate of all metaphysics, namely, the existence of a supra-sensible reality, is itself, therefore, not a proposition.[1]

We believe that in all this there is a false rigorism; or at all events an appearance of rigorism which may hold good for the positive sciences but not for metaphysics. On the one hand, as we have seen, metaphysics can have no intention of

[1] Cf. A. J. Ayer, in *The Revolution in Philosophy* (London, 1956), pp. 70–87.

describing the supra-sensible as though it were an object, since the supra-sensible is to be conceived only as a principle or ground; while, on the other, it is essential to know exactly what is meant by "verification". If, as the logical positivists contended, it is a question of an "experimental and sensible verification", the *petitio principii* is glaring. Further, the condition itself is unmeaning, because there is not and cannot be any "experimental" verification of what is not an object but rather a ground or principle. Actually there are many forms of verification, according to the kind of inquiry or field of knowledge we have in view. Verification is not to be understood in a purely univocal sense.

As against this, however, it could be urged that all such considerations are merely so much argument in face of the constant fact of the growing dispossession of philosophy by the sciences whether of nature or of man in the interest of an all-pervading positivism. We are here confronted, it is claimed, by a phenomenon which may be schematically described as follows: What philosophy continues to witness is the gradual occupation by the positive sciences of realms which were formerly exclusively its own. The old-fashioned philosophical logic has now been supplanted by "logistic"— a discipline strictly positive. Experimental psychology extends the field of its investigations ever further. The older conception of psychology as concerned, by right, with the relations of soul and body is today giving place to phenomenology, understood as a form of strictly positive knowledge. "Characterology" and sociology, thanks to their use of statistical methods, are similarly turning into fully-fledged sciences, again in the positivist's sense of the word. Morals itself, in part at least, now sees its terrain invaded by methods and procedures of an identical type.

It might, perhaps, be said in reply that at all events there remains to philosophy what used to be called the "philosophy of nature", or the whole region of *metempirical* knowledge, somewhere between the empirical sciences of nature and metaphysics proper. But what significance can this old-style philosophy of nature retain in the face of the developments of modern scientific knowledge? In this world *time* belongs to physics, space to both mathematics and physics, *life* to biology. What formerly was known as the "philosophy of the sciences"—the philosophy, as Berdyaev dubbed it, of those who knew no science—has fallen more and more within the province of science itself which now quite rightly assumes responsibility for devising its own theory—for there is an "epiphysics" just as there is an "epitheory" of logic.

Metaphysics in turn has found itself threatened. On the one hand, it is increasingly isolated from positive knowledge and therefore detached from experience, and so has come to be looked on as a purely gratuitous and arbitrary mode of thought. On the other, the positive sciences, in admitting no bounds to the field of their own researches and discovery, seem to assume for themselves what originally was the ambition of metaphysics alone—to preside, namely, over the entire realm of the knowable.

These views, repeatedly expressed in our day, compel us to reconsider the problem of metaphysics in a completely new light. Before doing so, however, it will be of help to introduce a point which at once very considerably restricts the scope of the objection. We are apt to speak of science and philosophy in general as though they were in themselves essentially unchanging and eternal. Now the truth is that they both of them change constantly and therefore the problem of their relations as constantly changes its form. No longer is it what it was in the days of Aristotle; nor is it even what it was fifty years ago. Tomorrow it will be different again. Actually the most striking contemporary fact seems to be a sort of reversal of the former order of things. This consisted in stating that the positive sciences are confined to the concrete and experimental, whereas metaphysics pertains to the rational and abstract. Nowadays the whole trend within the sciences is towards replacing this order by one quite different: science is becoming more and more rational, whilst philosophy turns increasingly to experience in its most concrete forms.

For the sciences which seem today to offer us the essential pattern of "scientific" knowledge—namely, mechanics and physics—show up more and more plainly as *rational* sciences, in which the observable is virtually swallowed up in the conceivable. In the middle of the last century thermodynamics provided the model for a hypothetico-deductive science. Electromagnetism, quantum physics, wave mechanics, in their turn, are following the same course. The positive sciences find increasing expression in mathematical terms, and the phenomena which they study can be adequately reduced to formulas of the same order. "The contemporary trend in science", it has recently been said,

> shows that progress of positive knowledge is much more the fruit of an expected consistency than of evidence experimentally tried. It might even be claimed that experience (or the evidence) is of no account until it has assumed the shape of a law, which in its turn has a clear meaning only when clothed in mathematical form, thus allowing prediction and a mathematical deduction of consequences. It could be affirmed that in general the advance of scientific knowledge appears as a kind of extension of the area of coherence and that rational organization has a more important and effective part in it than experimental verification. Chemical bodies proliferate by means of a rational *schema* and the laboratory outstrips nature. An unlimited mathematization thus offers to the principle of coherence an entirely new situation.[2]

The philosopher, no doubt, will still seek "something" behind these mathematical formulas; but for the physicist there is nothing: the phenomenon is wholly covered by the formula. Intuition no longer has any place. This process, pushed to its logical conclusion, would enable the entire physical world to be comprised in a single equation, thus achieving that ideal

[2] M. L. Roure, *Logique et Métalogique* (Paris and Lyons, 1957), p. 226.

of simplicity which inspires our men of learning. A good many sciences, biology, for example, are still largely "empirical", but it can be said that the aim of all of them is to become as consistently "rational" as mechanics and physics; to be transformed, that is, into hypothetico-deductive systems, expressed in metric formulas and constituting, as systems, an interconnected whole. Hence the universe of science, marvellously effective for all practical purposes, is becoming always more abstract and unreal.

Metaphysics, on the contrary, having had gradually to consign to the positive sciences an entire field of experience which once fell within its own province, now finds itself, as a result of this very reversal, confined to its true mission, which at times it has appeared to neglect in the interest of hazardous speculations, and to its proper realm—that of the *subject* as such: the subject, namely, which, because science is of its own constructing, itself lies outside the scope of science. It is this subject—man himself, that is—in its full and concrete reality, which it is the task of metaphysics to comprehend and define, whether as the creator of science, as the subject of duty or as the seeker after a world beyond that of science —a world, in short, in which are to be found the principle and meaning of all things. For it is impossible to explain the subject (i.e. man) without at the same time explaining the world as a whole. For although, from the standpoint of science, the subject is simply a "being-in-the-world", it can nevertheless transcend the world by the power of thought: both by thinking itself and (in so doing) by thinking the world which it constructs about itself. Thus it is that a new "philosophy of nature" and a new metaphysics come into existence with a claim to a degree of reality and concreteness to which the sciences cannot aspire.

These views do not diverge from the traditional ones in anything really essential and permanent. They may even have the additional advantage of reconciling that tradition with the contemporary scientific movement, by robbing of all meaning the problem of the relations of philosophy and the sciences as formerly envisaged, when conflict was considered to be not merely possible but inevitable. When Descartes, in a celebrated passage in his *Geometry*—an illustrative supplement to the *Discourse*—showed that the "real" sun is that not of ordinary perception but of mathematical physics, in which the imagination has no play, he in no way detracted from the importance of the *Cogito*—the subject as mind, that is—as lying outside analytic geometry and so forming the true province of philosophy and metaphysics. Ultimately the Cartesian conception is at one with those of Aristotle and St Thomas; or, to speak more precisely, it gives them their deepest and truest meaning as an inquiry into existence or, rather, the existent—Man or the Subject, in other words—and as thus establishing a science which is at once the most concrete, the freest and the highest. For this science—metaphysics—is *the* science *par excellence*, which, as the copingstone of all knowledge, provides the final justification of every other science.

This, however, may seem to be too sweeping and to conceal an initial prejudice in favour of metaphysics. The fact is, of course, that all such views run clean counter to what is now held by a great many present-day thinkers, especially in the English-speaking world, who remain on the whole faithful to the over-simplified positions of positivism. Especially are they opposed to popular views, dominated as these are by the enormous advances in the natural sciences. It is necessary, therefore, to reconsider the problem in another form. This is best done by means of a *reductio ad absurdum*, supposing, in conformity with positivist ideas, and pressing the argument to extremes, that Science will of itself be able to offer a complete account of reality. We refer to "Science" in order to signify either the unification of knowledge or the aggregate of the positive sciences—the only ones, according to this theory, which have any claim to the name. To avoid the abstraction "Science" we would prefer to say "the Scientist"

—the human mind, that is, as identifying itself with Science and therefore with a world which is now fully aware of itself. If this appears to be an extrapolation there is yet nothing inherently absurd about it (highly improbable though it may seem) and it has, in fact, been suggested by both philosophers and scientists.

Such as it is, the positivist hypothesis has at least the advantage of presenting the problem in all its rigour. Would there still be, on the supposition of a "complete" science, any place at all for metaphysics? Would there remain any irreducible residue for knowledge which could be looked on as metaphysical—as relating, that is, to an investigation and a cognitive technique absolutely different from that of Science (or the Scientist)? We believe that the answer would still have to be in the affirmative; and this for three main reasons, which could be summarized by saying that a Science supposedly complete would none the less carry with it a threefold problem—one of value, of thought and of existence. But all this needs to be argued as closely as possible.

VALUE

Science is positive knowledge; it is a formulation of general laws, and even, ultimately, of a single universal Law, such as would unify both phenomena as a whole and the particular laws which relate to phenomena. By definition these general laws, or the one universal Law, are simply *factual*; for they are the fact, as we have already said, of the World itself. From this point of view it may fairly be said that Science is from first to last a matter of the indicative. It thus takes no account whatever of the realm of laws properly so-called, the objects of which are *values* and which themselves create absolute *moral obligations*, or, in Kantian phrase, "categorical imperatives".

The question to be settled is whether Science has any authentic means of "explaining" values. Can *imperatives,* that is to say, be turned into *indicatives*, the moral law into facts? It is well known of course that, on the one hand, sociologists of the school of Durkheim, and, on the other, Marxists and existentialists of the Sartrean persuasion, maintain in their different though converging ways that such "explanation" is possible. To embark on a discussion of these views is not at the moment our concern, although we shall have to return to them later. But we may point out that they are all equally lacking in consistency and are indeed self-contradictory. For positivist sociology, Marxism and Sartrean existentialism themselves presuppose an *absolute of value* apart from which they would have no meaning. This, for Durkheim, is Society: the collectivity is the goal of the individual's secret intentions and the end to which his whole activity is directed. It is the absolute whence all else derives, and the God of the monotheistic religions is no more than its idealized expression. For Karl Marx the absolute is the Classless Society, in which the State will have "withered away" and the final advent of which will determine the categorical imperatives of a universal ethic. It is in the proletariat that this universalist vocation resides, the outcome of which, by a necessary dialectic, will be the State's eventual disappearance. The evidence for this, in Marx's eyes, is so clear that it amounts to a revelation of absolute value. For Sartre the absolute is that Freedom to which we all of us are "condemned". But at the same time, and by virtue of these same absolute values, there is a Good and an Evil, equally absolute, which no Science can either justify or explain away. For Science—and therefore the Universe—is itself subject to these values, which thus appear as at once *absolute and transcendent*.

One way out, however, would be to say that Value is the Universe itself, that the Universe is ultimate and all-comprehending Reason. The pursuit of our argument forbids us, for the moment, to question the *positive* element in this idea. But we must observe that the seemingly implied *negative* element, namely, the denial of any irreducible "beyond" to Science or the Universe, would here be a purely gratuitous postulate, such as would mean, in effect, an arbitrary identification of the Universe as *fact* with the Universe as *value*. Indeed, for the identification to be valid, we should have to maintain that every value is in the long run merely some given state of things, or, negatively, that there is no value beyond things. But these are typically metaphysical assumptions, and in any case have nothing "scientific" about them. For the affirmation that Science is the sole Value, or that it can with universal sufficiency define all values, is itself a *judgement of value* quite incapable of "scientific" demonstration. We should, in fact, have to explain the genesis of the idea of value itself on exactly the same lines; and in this nobody, so far, has succeeded. Theories which presume to do so all have the fatal defect of assuming the problem to be already solved, or else of advancing as a solution what is no more than a statement of the issue.

There is, however, a still more serious objection to the positivist hypothesis; and this is that Science, by continuing to develop without thought for human values, may become a threat to man himself, as the development of atomic physics has plainly shown. For Science does not supply its own rule or standard. In itself it is *indifferent to ends*, indifferent to the entire moral and human order. It thus needs to be governed and controlled by values outside itself, to which it is subordinate as the means to an end.

THOUGHT

Were we to suppose that Science and the Universe are essentially one—that Science is competent to provide a complete explanation of the Universe—it would still be necessary to point out that there is a "beyond" for both the Universe and Science: namely, the mind or thought which in some sense takes possession of the Universe or the totality of phenomena. Indeed, the *Subject* by whose action Science is built up necessarily lies outside Science and transcends it, were Science even to be regarded as "complete". "Scientific views," writes Merleau-Ponty, "according to which I am but a 'moment' in reality, are always both naïve and disingenuous, since they imply—though without saying so—that other view, the view of consciousness, by which reality first takes shape around me and thus begins to exist for me."[3] It is in fact utterly impossible to comprise Thought (or the Subject) in Science or the Universe merely as an *element* within it; otherwise there would be no science at all. The radical immanence of the Subject (or Thought) would exclude all distance between the Universe and itself and bring about an absolute coincidence between it and the flux of phenomena. There could, in a word, be neither Subject nor Thought.

Science, *ex hypothesi*, explains everything except the fact of Science itself. If consciousness is essentially "intentional" —if, that is, it is consciousness *of something* and not mere consciousness *per se*—it must have a corresponding object. This is a fact which science can ignore even less than philosophy; and for science this "object" is the Universe. The question that presents itself is whether the universe, as "global object", is really adequate to the full range and fundamental intentionality of consciousness. The answer, from the positivist standpoint, would clearly be that it is— an affirmation which itself defines the position which we are examining. However, it encounters the insurmountable obstacle of making the appearance of mind wholly inexplicable. In other words, it can account neither for *the fact of science itself* nor for that of *freedom*. If the animal cannot transcend its universe—if, as St Thomas says, it is "a form completely immersed in nature"—it is simply "because between it and its world the corrrespondence is so perfect that no hiatus or gap can be conceived by which it could escape it".[4] The object

[3] *Phénoménologie de la Perception*, p. 609.
[4] Stanislas Breton, *Conscience et Intentionnalité*, p. 261.

ʌas here a power so dominating and all-pervading that no
disjunction is possible by which the immersion could be
lessened or the smallest degree of freedom be gained. "If,
then, I can step outside the universe—and Science itself is
proof that I can—it is because the universe, while being
'consubstantial' with me—since in a sense I form part of it—
does not entirely comprehend me." The original intentionality, comprising as it does the possibility of a certain transcendence such as Science itself achieves, implies that its
object, being inclusive of the universe, is more than the universe.

The positivist doctrine, accordingly, has a double defect.
On the one hand, it fails to perceive that the idea of an
empirical "whole"—implied by that of a knowledge exactly
correspondent with the universe—is already a *metempirical*
idea*; one, that is, which is inconceivable at the level of a
purely positive knowledge, since this same "whole" or
totality can be thought of only as something which necessarily
transcends experience. On the other hand, it implicitly assumes the reality of a Subject which, in complete detachment
from experience, thinks of it as an object, thereby transcending it.

Thus the more we examine the positivist hypothesis the
more certain we become of the ultimate independence of a
dialectical process which can conceive nature because and
only because it is not itself merely a part of nature. But the
same conclusion is inevitable if we consider the matter from
another angle. The universe of phenomena brings us back to
mind, for the order which we discover or assume to exist
in phenomena implies an activity which is not itself inherent in
nature inasmuch as it somehow dominates nature. Science is
the product of mind, and without mind there could be no
science. Indeed, the Subject does not simply take possession
of nature by Science, but in a way *creates* nature itself. This
is true quite apart from any idealist doctrine; for leaving aside
all theories that might be thought to presuppose the solution

we are here seeking it can freely be admitted that the task of Science is not to be reduced to one simply of depicting its external data. It is neither a copy nor a photograph, even though it remains through and through objective and obedient to the facts of experience. Rather it is the world itself and the sum of its phenomena, but in a manner absolutely its own, not only because the Universe and Nature are brought by it into an abstract schematism, but also and mainly because the Universe acquires intelligibility only by means of the Thought which thinks it.

Physics itself, in every meaning of the word—whether the ancient one, as a "metempirical" understanding of the nature of reality, or the modern one, as positive knowledge of phenomena—is unquestionably one of the most striking proofs of man's metaphysical capacity. In fact, positivism is contradicted by it. If it is true, as Maurice Blondel says, that the world is a "cosmic thought", then such a "thought" is potential only and cannot actualize itself except by thought; so much is this the case that Thought seems more real to us than the Universe itself. For Thought envelops it and draws from it its full meaning—which is simply to say, once more, that it transcends it absolutely, since the "whole" cannot itself include the consciousness which reveals it nor the thought which "realizes" it. Positivism's cardinal error is in claiming to be a pure *objectivism*. But if it is mind which makes the universe possible—in the sense of becoming an intelligible reality—it cannot itself be a mere "thing" or object within the universe. We must recognize, then, once and for all, that there is a realm—of Mind or Thought—of which Science cannot take possession and which demands a mode of approach that is absolutely original and incapable of being assimilated to the methods of positive knowledge.

EXISTENCE

The consideration of being or existence leads us, still more radically, to the same conclusion. Why should there be "being" rather than nothingness? The question is one which forces itself upon the philosopher, though not on the scientist as such, for whom the universe is a *fact* or datum and no more. Here again, in face of the claims of a Science professing exact equivalence to a Universe fully understood, we can see that there is a realm of existence which necessarily is not open to the methods of the Scientist. Science has to do only with concrete things, as so many phenomena: the sheer *fact of being* is of no concern to it. Indeed, the Scientist, even if he hypothetically identifies himself with the Universe, cannot be present at his own birth: contemplation of his own coming into being is possible for no man. The World (along with himself) is already "there" when he sets out to learn about it and describe it. Science can understand particular births *within* the Universe, but the birth of the Whole remains a problem which, from its own standpoint, Science can neither pose nor resolve. The solution, to be at all possible, must be the work of a Reason capable of transcending the Whole. In a word, it has to be metaphysical.

By the metaphysical we do not, of course, mean merely the limit of the physical. Where that limit may happen to fall is of no consequence. As we have already stated, the vast spaces known to astronomy are really in no way different from the "infinitesimally small" of nuclear physics. Quantity as such undergoes no change of nature by either enlargement or diminution. Number, howsoever increased, is still number. There can be no ultimate "beyond" in the physical sense, since a physical "beyond" remains itself physical. Of "mystery" the physicist *qua* physicist knows nothing.

No doubt it could be denied at the outset that any question of existence is raised or that any solution of it of a metaphysical kind is therefore possible. Nevertheless, it is a fact and a universal fact that the question *is* raised; and the fact has a meaning. For it is not enough merely to write the question off as a factitious anthropomorphism. What is factitious is a particular way of answering the question; but a bad answer will not of itself dispose of a good question. Even if the fact that the question is constantly raised and continues to dominate both our metaphysical and our ordinary thinking be regarded as illusory, we still are faced with a further question no less complicated. The truth is that the problem of the existence of the Universe would not even occur if the Universe were of itself entirely capable of meeting our total capacity for knowledge. Science on any showing has neither the right nor the means of declaring the question of existence to be without significance or value, since, *ex hypothesi*, it identifies itself with the Universe and cannot go beyond it. The Scientist, utterly absorbed in a knowledge which, because of its perfection, he claims to be one with the Universe itself, may well find it odd that anyone should dispute the absolute sufficiency of the positive sciences; but this merely reveals the absurdity of a standpoint which would simultaneously both identify itself with the Universe and transcend it.

For Science to assert that the Universe has no meaning beyond itself and that none is to be looked for is thus to beg the whole question at issue. It is to deny, without the slightest attempt at proof, the very possibility of metaphysical knowledge. But metaphysics can establish the legitimacy of its own procedures by showing how the problem of the existence of the Whole necessarily arises *beyond* the point to which scientific knowledge can carry us. Indeed, if it is reason's task to discover the why and the wherefore of things, then the question of the *basic "why?"* is clearly implied in the structure of reason itself, as at the positive level science, too, makes use of it. For it is of the essence of all knowledge to *tend* towards an absolute knowledge. If the expressions of this tendency or fundamental need—universal and inherently characteristic of reason as it is—are infinitely varying and more or less direct, then science as a whole is nourished by it and dependent on it without ever being able fully to satisfy it. Metaphysics, on the contrary, is the theoretically adequate expression of an absolute knowledge and on this account is a true fulfilment of positive science.

Hence the question of the basic "why?" of existence can be evaded, or supposedly eliminated, only as the result of an essentially *anti-scientific* prejudice; since if Science has any meaning it is to explain the Universe and its organization, while at the same time the need for an all-comprehending intelligibility, characteristic of the positive sciences themselves, cannot be fulfilled by Science, inasmuch as the latter can do no more than identify itself with the Universe without being able to transcend it. Under pain of self-contradiction Science can only put itself, in order to achieve its proper ends, at the service of a further and a higher discipline—which is exactly what metaphysics is. Apart from this metaphysical demand, which in some obscure way is the motive force of Science itself, the latter would lose all real significance and end by being inconceivable. Absolute lack of curiosity would utterly destroy not only metaphysics but science as well.

There are, in fact, many scientists who still believe it necessary from the standpoint of science itself to deny that the problem of the existence of the Whole is a genuine problem, or at any rate that it is at all capable of being solved. Furthermore, philosophers of the neo-positivist school have tried, from the standpoint of positive knowledge in general, to explain the origin and growth of the idea of transcendence and thus to dispose of it as mere illusion. They contend that if knowledge of the universe is so far detachable from the Universe as to transcend it, it is because it harks back to its own source, because it coincides for a moment with the "event" and reaches a provisional totalization; for as there is always and necessarily an area outside present knowledge, or a certain "distance" of knowledge in relation to the universe, an illusion of transcendence soon creeps into philosophy, which believes itself to have discovered thereby a Logos (i.e. a Reason or Thought) superior to the Universe, whereas the

Universe is the *sole* Logos and has its absolute and final reason in itself.

Upon all this we may make two comments. The first relates to method and consists in noting that, first and always, we should have to show *by way of metaphysics itself* that the problem is not a genuine one or capable of being solved. Neither of the foregoing objections can be sustained on the basis of positive knowledge alone save at the cost of a *petitio principii*—to which, no doubt, a good many materialist thinkers are resigned, even though, nevertheless, it deprives their argument of any real weight. Thus in denying the legitimacy of metaphysics we should still have to engage in metaphysics. For however negative a metaphysic of negation may be it yet remains metaphysics. We must appeal, that is, to other principles and other methods than those of positive knowledge.

Secondly, an objection on the score of the origin and growth of the idea of transcendence, no matter how it is framed, boils down to the postulate that knowledge of the Universe—positive knowledge, when complete and wholly self-consistent, identical with the Universe, therefore—must at once dispose of metaphysics by simply depriving its problems of all meaning. But on the one hand this contention overlooks the fact that knowledge itself inevitably raises the whole question of metaphysics. This it does by the mere fact of its own "transcendence", since the very notion of a *Universe,* which positivism and phenomenology so naïvely assume, is already itself a metaphysical one. On the other hand, it would amount to giving to the term "transcendence" a connotation which by no means meets the requirements of the idea itself. For if it is true that the Universe always leaves us with further problems to solve and imposes on us a sense of "transcendence"—of a permanent "beyond" which Science's provisional schematizations cannot abolish—yet this "transcendence" could never be more than "horizontal". For a "horizontal" transcendence is transcendent *only* "as it were" inasmuch as its "beyond" would always be homogeneous with the "here–and–now"—with the physical, that is, indefinitely extended, not the *meta*physical. Even if we assume the abolition by Science of whatever vestige of "horizontal transcendence" may yet remain and assume, too, that Science has realized its ambition of achieving total knowledge, nevertheless the imperative demands of reason would still confront us with the problem of a *vertical* Transcendence—of the ultimate meaning of being as such.

Whence it follows that the question of existence remains on any hypothesis and its legitimacy is bound up with (so to say) its very situation, since, as we have seen, the mere act of our raising it already of itself implies the transcendence of thought and justifies it in its profoundest aims. Thus it is that Science, from its very nature, "forgets the existence of Being". Poetry, no doubt, seems able at times to console us "by producing, through imagination, that illusion of immanence which we call beauty". But the illusion is only short-lived and man cannot rest upon it permanently. As soon as he thinks seriously about the worlds of science and of art he becomes only too painfully aware of "the absence of Being". Hence the birth of metaphysics, which, from this angle, is at once both a "discourse on the absence" and a recovery of the presence of Being and its absolute conditions.[5]

Whatever answer we give to the question of existence— whether we attempt to assume the reality of a Logos wholly immanent in the Universe or of a Reason creative of the world—it must necessarily give rise to *reflection* about the Universe; a reflection which, once again, has to be distinguished from Science and which, strictly speaking, is metaphysical. Science is entirely concerned with objectivity. Reflection on the Universe, however we conceive it, means a contemplation of both it and Science as it were from above. It implies a transcendence of a completely different kind, a *vertical* one, whether theist or pantheist. That is why it is

[5] F. Alquie, *Philosophie du Surréalisme* (Paris, 1955), p. 215.

correct to say that "it is in affirming transcendence that man discovers his most authentic truth"[6]; though the question would remain whether a pantheistic transcendence meets all the requirements of a genuine Transcendence. This, however, we have no need to dwell on here, as we have already done so in another volume in this series.[7] All we have to establish is that, no matter what one's viewpoint may be, the problem of existence is inevitable, that it is not a question of "positive" knowledge merely, and that as regards Science it calls for an investigation of an entirely new sort: one which is essentially metaphysical.

We have thus shown, we believe, that although Science is unquestionably a mode of truth it is not and cannot be the sole mode. A metaphysic, therefore, is always necessary, for it has its own special problems which Science can neither pose nor resolve by the methods proper to it. These problems would still persist in a way incapable of statement in any other terms even were the sum of all positive knowledge to be attained. They are, as we have seen, the problems respectively of Thought, Being and Value, and together constitute metaphysics' own inalienable realm. That we cannot express them in any other terms, nor doubt their legitimacy or even their necessity, springs from the very fact that science, considered in all its formal rigour and in its widest scope—for in its own province it knows no limitations—so far from getting rid of them, compels us to ponder them with an even greater realization of their urgency and imperious demand. Apart from metaphysics there can be no hope of discovering the meaning and significance of either man or the universe.

The whole of this discussion is far from being merely negative. On the contrary, it has initiated us little by little into the precise meaning of metaphysical science and has familiarized us with many of its main features and aspects. But this by itself is not enough. We now must attempt to

[6] Alquie, *op. cit.*, p. 211.
[7] No. 15, *The God of Reason*, pp. 90–7.

define and specify, in a fittingly schematic form, the chief problems of metaphysics and the solutions that these seem to call for in the context of a philosophy which, while in one sense Christian, seeks, in another, to be as strictly rational as possible. No doubt, as should be clear from everything we have said, metaphysics has really but one problem: that of the Absolute. But this Absolute, whose presence in us and in the universe we apprehend by the very dynamism which impels us to seek it, nevertheless reveals its presence only by the mediation of other absolutes—"relative absolutes" pertaining to some particular order or realm and witnesses by reason of their absolute character (and by means of analogy) to the existence and the nature of the Principle or Absolute which is in no way relative. These other absolutes testify to the existence of an Absolute which falls outside any single order of being, out-tops all levels of rational intelligibility.

Such are the conclusions which form the proper object of natural theology, or *theodicy*, as it is often nowadays called. They are dealt with in another volume of the present series and so need not be discussed again here, save only as they may support or illustrate our argument. The domain of metaphysics, in so far as it is to be distinguished from theodicy (which actually constitutes the major part of it) is therefore that of the relative-absolutes of which we have already spoken under the three headings of *thought*, *being* and *value*, and which are the objects, respectively, of three distinct studies: psychology, ontology and axiology.

We have now to consider these three aspects of the general problem of the absolute in order to note what problems of a less general kind each may involve. Our aim is not of course to offer a treatise on metaphysics but simply to indicate the meaning of the most important questions which the metaphysician encounters in these three fields.

CHAPTER V

EPISTEMOLOGY AND PSYCHOLOGY

What, accordingly, are the problems which present themselves to the metaphysician when confronting the irreducible facts of thought and mind? They can be ranged under the successive headings of intelligence, language, freedom and the spirituality of the soul.

REASON AND LANGUAGE

In modern psychology the term *intelligence* has been given a greatly enlarged scope, even to the point of including animal behaviour. If in its widest sense it denotes the capacity to solve problems, then animals, thanks to their instinct, display a form of intelligence which is quite astonishingly accurate. But in their case it soon becomes evident that this intelligence is a property of instinct and not a faculty of the animal itself. By contrast, man, who, as compared with the animals, is but poorly equipped with instinctive techniques, has an infinitely greater range of needs which have to be met in constantly changing ways and by means of a specific capacity for invention and adaptation. What is called civilization or culture is nothing else than an enormously complex assemblage of adjustments whereby man is able to tackle the countless problems raised by his bodily and spiritual needs alike. From the very beginning mankind appears essentially to have been a species which poses and solves problems by means of the instruments which it continues to produce with inexhaustible ingenuity. Thus viewed, man, as Bergson says, can be characterized as a tireless maker of tools: *homo faber*.

Intelligence has features, then, that are wholly confined to man. As a capacity for grasping a given situation—for perceiving, that is, the relations subsisting between a collection of data, for choosing, between possible solutions, the one which best promotes the desired aim, and, lastly, for directing behaviour to an end by a series of teleological adjustments, the human intelligence is primarily a *capacity for mental organization* which consciously sets itself objectives and which, in order to attain them, conjures up a limitless variety of means. As a result humanity, unlike the animal creation, escapes the bondage of the present, transcends space and time, and detects ever new kinds of necessary relationships. Of this liberation and transcendence language, as the expression of thought, is the clearest sign.

Thus as between even the highest of the animals and man himself, even uncivilized man, there are two essential differences to be noted. The latter, in his mental representations and his actions, escapes the confinement of immediate sensory data. He can freely conjure up mental pictures, form general ideas independent of present sense-impressions, and direct his actions according to a considered plan. Further, he has the power of opposing his instinctive tendencies. It is this which, grounded as it is in the rational intelligence, constitutes the very essence of his freedom.

In short, it is man's distinctive privilege, thanks to his mental endowment, to be able to dominate both the world and himself, a privilege which nowadays is usually defined by the term *reason*, or the *faculty of the absolute*, as exercised in the search for grounds and causes. It is this faculty or function which characterizes the intelligence in its properly human form and makes it necessary for us, as we have seen, to transcend the data—supposedly full and sufficient—offered us by science, and to base value, thought and being in the absolute.

In fact this search for grounds and causes, this resort to principles, accompanies the awakening of the intelligence, as the child's repeated "why?" and "how?" are enough to show, since they are the metaphysical phenomenon in embryo. This insistent need for explanation is the essential expression of reason, which is defined chiefly in terms of *reasoning* only because it is a search for causes and principles. Such a search is spontaneously induced in us by the idea or feeling that *everything has its raison d'être*, and again, *that being alone explains being* and renders it intelligible. In this sense what is called the "principle of reason" is also the principle of universal intelligibility, under the three aspects of causality, finality and substance. This principle, together with the absolutely basic one of non-contradiction (which states that "a thing cannot at once and in the same respect both be and not be"), is operative in all metaphysics and is the foundation of the whole of rational theology. Self-evident, necessary and universal, both objectively and subjectively, first principles are implied in every activity of the mind, and the "metaphysical phenomenon" is but the spontaneous expression of the objective requirements, inherent in the relation of mind to being, which they disclose.

Language is the clearest token of the metaphysical play of reason. It is indeed, primarily and intrinsically, the expression of a self spontaneously affirmed as subject in opposition to the objects of its experience. As such it is, in origin, the effect and the sign of a liberation and an autonomy as regards mere things. From another angle, and contrary to what obtains in the animal world, where mimicry and the cry are the result simply of blind natural impulse, man's self-expression is already weighted with a more or less explicit *intentionality*.* Language, accordingly, declares the meaning which man seeks to attach to the world, and this intentionality is itself the consequence of the liberation which self-expression implies. Finally, it is the act whereby man communicates with other subjects in order to realize, along with them, his chosen ends, and thus to fulfil his autonomy. Language and society are necessarily coexistent and exercise a reciprocal causality.

The impersonality and universality of language are the conditions of the *intersubjective communication* wherein is achieved that fulness of "active transcendence" in relation to the world which is the very definition of man's humanity. Unquestionably, as a result of such depersonalization, language loses its immediate relationship to the image itself, which lies of course at the root of all naming; it inevitably assumes, therefore, a somewhat artificial and conventional appearance. Attempts have even been made to present this artificiality or neutrality as an ideal in comparison with the original imagery. This, however, is to misunderstand the phenomenon of linguistic "socialization". The latter is, in fact, no more than a transitory phase between the imagination whence the word derives and the convention in which its expressive value becomes lost. Indeed, language has meaning only in so far as it retains its contacts with the creative power of the image. Cut off from this the words grow old and die. To survive and have life in them they must receive some access of expressive energy. The life of society thus imposes on language a permanent tension as between the neutrality of the actual sign of which it makes use and the wealth of imagery by which a word's vitality is assured. And it is precisely this tension which gives rise to *linguistic history*. The ambiguity is never likely to be removed, but its meaning may be grasped when we rediscover in language the twofold aspect of (*a*) a *creation* which, by process of naming, both brings the world into being and affirms the subject, and (*b*) an *intersubjectivity* which is effective only through the mediation of the universal and the impersonal.

FREEDOM

Freedom is the child of reason. Conceptual language, when analysed in terms of all that it implies, already indicates, as we have just seen, man's ability to view things from a distance, to escape their immediate grasp, mentally to set in order the entire field of his action, and finally, to become the master of his own behaviour. All this it is to which we give the name of freedom, here understood not only as a *freedom to act*—freedom, that is, from external constraint—but *freedom to will*—that deliverance from internal compulsions which is most clearly exercised in man's necessary choice between good and evil, or between the different kinds of good which present themselves to him on the course of his existence.

The time-honoured discussions to which free-will, or the power of auto-determination, has given rise have not in any way altered the essential elements of the problem. The sense of moral freedom common to all men, along with the allied and dependent sense of personal moral responsibility, is so profound that no objection has ever succeeded in throwing serious doubt on it or in reducing it to mere illusion. Even for our contemporary existentialists freedom is a sort of immediate datum in so far as it constitutes the very essence of man. Such at least is Sartre's position. Man, he tells us, is "condemned to be free": the choice of his ends resting with himself, he is wholly unconditioned, without reason or justification for being; and he can no more deprive himself of this choice than he can refuse *to be*—which would, in fact, be merely another way of choosing to be.

This line of argument, questionable though it is in the form which it here assumes, is not without a certain basis in that recognition of the metaphysical demand for freedom which is inherent in the very structure of our human existence. In a way, indeed, it is quite true that man is "condemned to be free", since freedom is an essential property of the rational being that he is. Man is free by virtue of the fact that he is man and that he exists, and were he able to give up his freedom such abdication would itself remain an achievement of freedom. Nevertheless the expression, "condemned to be free", has on Sartre's lips a dubious significance, since it implies that in man there is so absolute a contingency as to the choice of his ends that his freedom in respect of them becomes intrinsically "absurd". We believe, on the other hand, that if freedom is an aspect of reason and hence is of the essence of man's nature, it is, as such, the instrument by which man realizes himself *as rational*—brings into existence, that is to say, by his own effort and according to the norms of reason, a unique essence which also must be his most personal achievement. Man is not "condemned" to freedom as though in consequence of some accident to which he is obliged to submit without comprehending its meaning. He ought rather to *acquiesce* in his freedom—in reason itself, that is, since reason is at once its foundation and its law.

It remains that freedom, certain as a fact, raises a good many metaphysical problems in its actual exercise. If the conception which would reduce it to a state of balance or impartiality between the varying motives which beset it has seemed generally incompatible with its true nature, this is because it implies a sort of will-mechanism that can hold good only of automata moving according to the laws governing the equilibrium of forces. Rather does freedom appear as *self-determining power*. It is man who wills by his volition, and if there is a freedom of willing it is that of man himself. In other words, if it is certain that there is not and cannot be a free act that is without motive—since such an act would be irrational, devoid of adequate grounds—the motive itself could not be conceived as the *cause* of the act, inasmuch as causality would then imply the determinism which presides in the world of mere objects. Motive, in reality, is integral to a free act; more precisely, it establishes it as free. To be free is, properly speaking, to make a motivated act; and this it is which is connoted by the term "auto-determination", the meaning of which, in the case of the rational subject, is the power to be what he himself wills to be. A truly free act is always something other than what is explicable by a purely

external cause; but it cannot be other than it is in the eyes
of him who has willed the spiritual and moral order or being
whence it proceeds and which at the same time it reveals. As
for the ultimate source of this power of being oneself, it is
reason as such, by which, as we have seen, man both liberates
himself from bondage to sense and becomes capable of taking
possession of himself by reflective thought.

THE SOUL AS SPIRIT

It is this power of reflection, of returning upon the self,
which, in all metaphysical systems and in any explanation of
it, is the basis of the claim that the soul is a spiritual reality.
Reason and freedom are themselves but its properties; they
pertain, that is, to a soul which not only is immaterial—for
so too is that of an animal—but which in its essential being
and highest functions is finally independent of the bodily
organism. It is in the first place by the spirituality of his soul
that man is the metaphysical animal which we have analysed,
a being, that is, who, in himself and by virtue of an ultimate
and irreducible difference from the rest of nature, belongs to
the realm of spirit.

This reality, this relative independence of the soul has been,
in the course of the centuries, the subject of a concretizing
mythology, the soul being depicted sometimes as a "double"
of the body, sometimes as a sort of thin air or breath. But the
images employed always betray the spiritual reality which
they seek to express. We still speak, even in the most refined
metaphysical language, of "soul" and "spirit", words which
etymologically originate in crude and woefully inadequate
analogies. But, on the one hand, knowing that the actual
expression fails to embody the full meaning and that the
intention behind it is more than the mere word, we can take
care not to be misled by the dubious materiality of the image,
and, on the other, the terms "soul" and "spirit", as used by
philosophers, have lost all their animistic associations and

signify a reality that excludes all representation. The spiritual soul is not indeed a thing which can be located and hidden, so to speak, in a body, nor even, as in Plato, conceived of as the pilot of a ship—although this particular analogy is still perfectly sound as a means of expressing the soul's function as governor and guide. The Aristotelian tradition, which in a number of respects has adopted the existential phenomenology of our own day, maintains that the soul is the "form of the body". By this we are to understand it as that by which the body exists *as a human body* and consequently that it is identifiable, in one aspect, with the body which it animates, since together they constitute a single substance or *a single being*, complex, no doubt, but a unity nevertheless. It is not therefore a matter of "here" or "there", nor does it occupy (as Descartes suggested) the pineal gland, or the heart, or any physical organ. It is present everywhere—"everywhere" signifying, however, something neither exact nor strictly appropriate; for the word itself implies space, whereas the soul is "spatial" only accidentally, in so far as it is the form of a physical body and accords it existence as such.

Although the form of the body, however, and hence bound to the body through which it exercises its animal functions, the soul, because of its properly spiritual functions of rationality, reflection and freedom, clearly transcends the physical frame and its mechanisms. For the universality of reason is no more compatible with a radical reduction of matter to the mere succession of its states than is the rational ordering of freedom to be reconciled with the determinism of natural phenomena; nor can the return upon and possession of the self by reflection be harmonized with a matter the basic property of which is to be divisible into mutually exclusive parts occupying space. The human soul, by virtue of what constitutes it as *spiritual*, is therefore independent of the body and is endowed by nature with immortality.

In opposition to this we encounter, throughout the history of thought from Epicurus and Lucretius in antiquity to

Marxism in our own day, a whole cluster of arguments bearing the general name of *materialism*. It certainly is curious that in this respect man should have been so ready to deny his spiritual nature. But, on the one hand, this same materialism, being itself a reflective theory, is inevitably self-contradictory in that it is already a proof of spirituality to be capable at all of doubting that of the soul, since in a materialist context such doubt would in fact be wholly inconceivable; and, on the other hand, the materialist contention affords the most usual pretext both for the "common-sense" notion of the soul as a "thing"—for, whether we are metaphysicians or not, it is always *images* which spring most naturally and forcefully to mind—and for a number of theories, like those of Plato and Descartes, who in their eagerness to "explain" the mystery of the relationship between body and soul succeed in doing so only too well, reducing it to a condition which in fact abolishes it or renders it unintelligible. Materialism relies on specious arguments which generally turn out to be based on mere absurdities.

Marx and Engels themselves considered that it was impossible to fall back on the sort of position which they called "vulgar materialism", as expressed by writers like Helvetius[1] and Cabanis.[2] No experimental investigation, the latter tell us, will enable us to discover in the human body anything other than organized matter. Now it is clear enough that in the body there is only organized matter and that if the soul is immaterial it could not be reached by material means. Another argument—La Mettrie's—is that "organized matter is endowed with a principle of motion which alone differentiates it from that which lacks it and that with animal life everythng depends on the diversity of this organization".[3] Or again, we have Holbach's view that "movement is a mode of being which necessarily proceeds from the essence of matter

[1] *De l'homme* (1772).
[2] *Rapports du physique et du moral dans l'homme* (1802).
[3] *L'homme-machine*, p. 68.

itself".[4] On the strength of this principle Cabanis declared that "the brain causes the secretion of thought organically". But these are all purely gratuitous assertions without any shadow of proof. In fact, the organization of matter is not an effect of chance and cannot be explained apart from some immanent governing principle, while to say that the brain "secretes thought" is really no answer at all and begs the whole question at issue.

As for the familiar argument of a psycho-physical parallelism, it can in no way prove that psychological phenomena—least of all spiritual—are produced by the bodily organisms. For the facts of correspondence, which are certain and evident enough, could themselves justify only the statement that there is a *relation* between the two series, the psychological and the physiological, and nothing more. What that relation actually is would still have to be determined. Psychology, however, makes it clear that it cannot be a *causal* one and that it would moreover be unintelligible for a physical or chemical mechanism to produce thought, create freedom and provide a basis for reflection. It is impossible, in short, for anything to produce just anything whatsoever.

Indeed it is evident that materialism reduces all conscious activity to a merely *mechanical model*. The *petitio principii* becomes immediately apparent. Attempts, however, are made in our day to justify this mechanistic point of view by instancing the achievements of the electronic brain. But the latter hardly helps us, since although it can perform the most astoundingly complicated operations with a virtually infallible skill it is itself but the expression and product of thought. What it shows is that the human brain makes use of extremely complex mechanisms, a fact which, if it is true that the soul is the "form" of the body and that the body is an expression of the soul, goes without saying. It does not prove that these mechanisms are a chance concatenation and still

[4] *Système de la nature*, p. 22.

less that they function of their own accord, any more than it proves that the electronic brain is capable of building itself or of setting itself in motion.

Is the dialectical materialism of Karl Marx any more successful in its attempt to justify a materialist conception of man? This is what Engels sought to establish. Such a materialism, he contends, rests on

> the great and fundamental idea according to which the world ought not to be considered as a complex of *things* complete in themselves, but as one of *processes* in which things apparently stable, quite as much as their intellectual reflections in the brain (i.e. ideas), undergo constant change, coming to be, and passing away; and in which at last, and despite all seeming hazards and momentary reversals, a progressive development comes to light.

Such is the basic thesis of historical materialism. But it would be a grave mistake to suppose that this "scientific" materialism, as Marx and Engels are pleased to call it, differs in any essential respect from what they refer to as its "popular" counterpart. The fact is that the dialectic really makes no difference to it. Sartre, as is well known, has afforded us an energetic refutation of Marxist materialism.[5] He submits it to a cross-examination designed to expose its internal contradictions; for, as he says, all materialism must in principle exclude resort to any sort of metaphysical being. Yet in doing precisely this the materialist has already launched out into metaphysics, since if he reproaches "idealists" with having an unwarrantable metaphysical intention when they reduce matter to spirit, by what miracle will he avoid the same offence when he in turn reduces spirit to matter?

But there are more direct means of refutation open to us; we may start with one which underlines the implicit contradiction in the materialist account of consciousness. For con-

---

[5] "Matérialisme et Révolution", in *Situations* (Paris, 1949) III, pp. 135–225.

sciousness, in a materialist context, is little less than a scandal. It ought therefore to be got rid of and to that end reduced to matter. Accordingly it will have to be regarded as a mere thing or object among all the other things or objects that make up the world. But this in fact is unthinkable, both in principle and in the sort of form which the argument usually takes. For the principle consists in an explanation of consciousness by means of something external to it, which clearly amounts to postulating the materialist solution without making the slightest attempt to prove it, since if it is true that consciousness alone is capable of "explaining" things then any explanation must itself presuppose consciousness.

On the other hand, to reduce consciousness to a mere object among other objects is only to revert to an obsolete "epiphenomenalism"*, with all its inconsistencies and contradictions. Thought, as a product of consciousness considered simply as an object, would be no more than a "reflection" or epiphenomenon. But in what way are we to understand that this "reflection" reflects the sum of all objects? How is it that it has a breadth of scope infinitely greater than the object whence it proceeds? Moreover, such reflection, regarded as the datum of consciousness, must needs be adequately determined: every *effect* is strictly measured by the cause which produces it or by the sum of the conditions in which it is produced. Yet what could be more at variance with the spontaneity of consciousness and thought? "If the psychic fact is rigorously conditioned by the biological", writes Sartre,

and the biological, in turn, by the physical state of the world, I clearly see that the human consciousness can express reality in the way that an effect expresses its cause, but not in a way that a thought expresses its object. For how could a captive reason, ruled from without and guided by the chains of a blind causality, remain *reason* at all? How should I believe in the principles of my deductions if it is only an external event that causes me to have them—if, in Hegel's phrase, "reason is a bone"? By what chance can the mere brute outcome of circumstance offer us, at the same time, the keys to Nature?[6]

The truth is that where consciousness and thought are concerned we are already a long way from the merely physical and mechanical and are quite definitely in contact with an order essentially different.

But might not materialism become a more plausible doctrine if presented in a "dialectical" form? To assume so would be utterly unwarranted, for the simple reason that the very concepts of *materialism* and *dialectic* are incompatible. For in no way at all can the spatial relations of objects—relations, that is, in which objects are external to one another and mutually exclusive—be assimilated to relations created by the movement of dialectic. Dialectic is essentially a movement of ideas implying progress by successive syntheses through a continuous assimilation of the related terms, a movement tending, that is, towards the final constitution of a *whole* which can be looked on as the term, whether provisional or final, of the entire dialectical process. The latter can be understood only as implying a tendency of the whole towards self-realization and therefore as a sort of idea in act, internally impelling the successive stages of the movement towards the whole to be realized.

The truth is that nothing is more alien to or less to be reconciled with the order of spatial relations, in which the absolute rule is not the simultaneous transcending and conservation of a previous term but the mutual exclusion of all intervening terms. One may try no doubt to imbue matter itself with the momentum of dialectical progression. But this can be done only at the price of a confused and contradictory notion of what matter really is, conferring on it a kind of internal elasticity such as it in no way possesses. In fact, the materialist constructions of the Marxists, by which we pass

[6] *Op. cit.*, p. 143.

from the order of matter to that of life and thence to those of "spirit" and history, merely beg the question throughout. You start off by crediting matter with potential possession of the entire wealth of being, which it is supposed to produce from its own depths; but actually you never find in it more than you have already put there, for you can no more "draw" from it "spirit" or history or life than a conjurer can "draw" a rabbit from a hat unless he has first put it there. Matter is dark, opaque, passive, and as such incapable of dialectic. Its proper condition is one, if not of immobility, at least of total inertia. We may conclude from this that dialectical materialism is really an absurdity.

However, the refutation of materialism will not serve to validate, under the name of "spiritualism", a sort of "angelism" which by its exaggerations has invariably played materialism's own game. The body is not a simple phenomenon and is more than a mere instrument of the soul. Actually it is the expression and manifestation of the soul, so deeply and closely conjoined with it that the two constitute a single reality. To fathom the nature of this unity is of course a tantalizing mystery, since our natural impulse is always to think in terms of things. But before being a mystery it is, first of all, a fact and on this account we can subscribe to the tardy wisdom of Descartes, who warns us to hold to an experience which nothing, in truth, will permit us either to set aside or to explain in full.

Metaphysical man most fully realizes himself in his ineradicable conviction that he belongs to the world of spirit and enjoys therefore a *personal immortality*. If indeed there is within man some principle which transcends matter and thus escapes the limitations of space and time, and which also thinks in terms of the universal and aspires to infinite goodness and happiness, then this principle itself cannot share the body's destruction, whether directly or, as in the case of the souls of animals, indirectly. It is, of itself, incorruptible and immortal. Personal immortality alone meets the absolute exigency of a being conscious of itself as a free, personal intelligence, subject, on that account, to the law of duty; a being whom death cannot extinguish or absorb, after an interval of "survival", in the anonymity of the Whole without at the same time frustrating its most natural and deep-seated aspirations. Were it not otherwise the moral order would lose at once all meaning and value.

We can now understand how metaphysical experience is also a *spiritual experience*, and how the latter, when it is developed in accordance with its full meaning and its full requirements is also a *religious experience* of which the mystical experience is only the perfection. Everything here is bound together by a logic whereof the saint alone achieves full awareness. The esotericism of so many of our psychologists, who in failing to realize that the psychic life is never more than surface-show, or at most but sign and symbol, deny to the mystical life all human truth, displays at once a lack of psychological insight and an ignorance of the real character of man. For the metaphysician must admit that if, between the ordinary experience which it is his business to interpret and one that is spiritual and mystical, there is always a gulf which his strictly ratiocinative thinking cannot bridge, then the very dynamism of an interior life deepened by charity tends spontaneously towards that beyond in which man both loses and finds himself, as St Augustine puts it, in a God "who is more intimate to me than the most intimate part of myself and higher than what is highest in myself".

Thus in height and depth mind penetrates all things and calls us to partake of its infinity. For not only is there infinity in the finite, but this infinity cannot achieve self-realization, as it were, save in another dimension, beyond the shapes and horizons of the world. It is to it as living and life-giving Love that in the final resort we must always appeal. In the words of Dante, Love is the truth alike of the world and of man.

CHAPTER VI

ONTOLOGY AND THEODICY

REALISM AND IDEALISM

The group of problems which constitute the subject-matter of Ontology, or the science of being *qua* being, can be reduced to two basic inquiries: one into the meaning of *being as such*—a question, that is, as to its intelligible structure; the other into *reason* or *primary cause*.

As to the first, it is evident that there is not and cannot be any real definition of being. For to define a thing is to bring it under some *genus*, while noting the *differentia* which distinguishes it within this *genus*. Thus we may say that man is an animal (*genus*) which is rational (*specific differentia*). Now being is not a *genus*, since there is nothing "outside" it, and whatever would be required to distinguish it is itself being and necessarily so. Being, therefore, is the primary and absolute datum from which we have to set out; or, more precisely, in which we have reflexively to establish ourselves. This is essentially a matter of analysis, which, as we have already shown, enables us to grasp within being as given in experience—and this, as such, is being-for-me—the absolute reasons for being simply *qua* being. Actually, being is always some particular being qualified and determined in this way or that; and being simply *qua* being—in the abstract or transcendental* meaning of the term—exists only in the mind and, because of its sheer "generosity", the infinite potential multiplicity of its content, in a form necessarily vague.

Upon this philosophers are, on the whole, in agreement. The real difficulty lies elsewhere and can be formulated in terms of the apparent dilemma between realism and idealism; which, contrary to what Karl Marx supposed, is not to be confused with that of materialism and spiritualism, to which we have alluded above. Schematically, the problem which metaphysical speculation has always to face is that of deciding whether being is a thing or an idea. To common sense, of course, the problem must seem absurd. But it cannot be ignored, once we start to question ourselves about the conditions and nature of our experience. In fact, the world of things exists and, in a sense, can only exist by and for the thought which thinks it and which, in thinking it, confers being upon it according to the truth of its inherent meaning. If, *per impossibile*, we abstract or parenthesize thought the world simply disappears and returns to the chaos of brute existence —to a "matter", that is to say, which is no more than a range of possibilities. From this point of view, therefore, being is *par excellence* thought or idea, and the universe of things reduces itself to the thought which gives it existence: that is, enables it to acquire meaning and value. All the great philosophies from Descartes onwards have adhered, under one guise or another, to that *idealism* which Le Roy well summarizes as comprising "two allied and complementary tendencies: one making nature depend on, or even reducing it to, thought— basing and absorbing being in thought; the other recognizing in thought, in its turn, a primacy of value, while at the same time seeking this value from the side of mind rather than of sense—from the side, as we may say, of 'inventive action' ".[1]

Opposed to this is the *realism* which seems to characterize ancient and medieval thought more than modern and which would present to thought a consistent universe of things with which it has to effect a harmony, *truth* being the conformity of thought with what is real. Such "realism" certainly fits in with the "evidences" the underlie the assertions of common

[1] *Essai d'une philosophie première* (Paris, 1956), I, p. 39.

sense which, however naïve it may be in its spontaneous expression, would be exceedingly difficult to repudiate altogether. In fact, say the defenders of realism, rationalist idealism tends to turn the world of experience into a sort of phantom or dream, even when, simultaneously, it seeks to present it as a "coherent whole"; as equally, if it wants to avoid falling into solipsism,* it tends to look for justification in a more or less explicit pantheism that not only solves nothing but actually adds to its difficulties.

The debate between idealism and realism, which has provided food for a three-centuries-old controversy, seems to derive, as we today are coming more and more clearly to realize, from a pseudo-problem. For the fact is that neither idealism nor realism is capable of a complete self-justification, nor can the one even arrive at a properly intelligible statement of its own position except by relying on and appealing to the other. That being exists and that the universe is a real universe is a basic datum which no idealist doctrine has ever succeeded in effectively questioning. If Berkeley, by his criticism of the notions of matter and substance, reduces the world to a series of ideas, so that, in the words of his famous formula, *esse est percipi*, then the world of ideas itself, as he conceives it, possesses the full objectivity and reality (as well as much more besides) which naïve realism attributes to the data of sense-perception. And when Brunschvicg, following Fichte, has to admit that knowledge necessarily begins with a "shock"—with, that is, a paradoxical encounter with something other than and radically different from mind—he introduces, whether intentionally or not, a *de facto* realism into an idealism which purports, nevertheless, to be thoroughgoing.

To this difficulty, which has often been pointed out, Brunschvicg is content to reply that "the human mind, since its first appearance and from the time when it becomes aware, in scientific knowledge, of its creative power, recognizes that it is freed from the order of matter and life" and that "it

would amount to self-betrayal were it to allow itself to become anything lower than what it is."[2] But is this answer
sufficient? If idealism is true (and in this lies all its truth)
the mind—or, more precisely, Mind—must account for all
things; and if there is "something below it" for which it cannot and need not account, then idealism makes an illogical
compact with a "realism" of the most implausible kind, in-
ferior even to the crude realism which, in dispensing with
theory altogether, at least confines itself—however inadequate
its explanations may be—to establishing data that can in no
way be denied: namely, that being *is*, that mind is not the
only reality and that there are "things" of which it must take
account. For the deepest and most genuine sense of philosophical realism consists in admitting both that there are
things which do not exist in virtue of the human mind alone
and that it is the latter's task to raise them to its own level
by giving them meaning and value. In saying this we are not
trying to unite—as does Brunschvicg when he states that
"the dualism of being and thought is definitely primitive and
irreducible"[3]—an idealism and a realism each pretending to
ignore the other; what we have in mind is a realism which
is at the same time an idealism and an idealism which likewise is a realism. This is the view to which Rosmini and
Lachelier give the name of "objective idealism". This, too,
it is which Sartre, among others, seems drawn to in seeking,
quite rightly, to escape the realist–idealist dilemma. "If", he
writes, "we are conscious of anything, it is necessary in the
first place that this 'something' should have a *real* being";[4]
that is, if we understand him correctly, that it should partake
of being in the realist sense of the word. Here, then, is an
evidence on which we can rely. But Sartre now pushes his
realism far beyond what is required, for he makes it clear
that the "something" which has "*real* being" must be "*un-*

[2] *Bulletin de la Société française de philosophie*, 1928, p. 24.
[3] *La modalité du jugement*, p. 98.
[4] *L'Être et le Néant*, p. 586.

related to consciousness";[5] and this seems to imply that relationship to consciousness would exclude the reality of being. Now there is nothing more questionable, as we have argued above in discussing Merleau-Ponty's views on the subject of being-as-it-is-for-me. If we were obliged to adhere to Sartre's definition, the realism envisaged by it would be a realism of the crudest and least acceptable kind. It would, in fact, be unintelligible. Such, too, is the type of realism which fits in with Sartre's idea of being-as-it-is-in-itself—something "thick, dark, opaque, and self-enclosed," wholly without relations either internal or external, something absurd and eternally *de trop*.[6]

But it is a view altogether too simple and crude which would have us believe in a universe independent of thought and subsisting in the impenetrability of its own being, entirely apart from any mind for which it might exist. The medieval realists, decidedly "realistic" though they were, entertained no such notion as this. By comparison they were virtually idealists. For in the first place the universe appeared to them as a prodigiously varied expression of the divine creative thought, and the very knowledge by which we gradually take possession of it can consist, in their view, only in re-encountering in things themselves the ideas from which they proceed and which in some manner they express. The universe as thus conceived is still, therefore, a universe of ideas; so much so that we might say that, in the world as it offers itself to our perception, mind—or what is analogous to mind—is apprehensible by mind. Plato, according to St Augustine, understood this perfectly, but without also understanding—through lack of the light which we owe to the Christian revelation—that the ideas by which the world was made and which impart to all things their meaning, subsist in the divine Word, "by whom all things were made".

It is true, nevertheless, that even this radical and universal

[5] *Ibid*. The italics are Sartre's own.
[6] *Ibid*., p. 23 f.

idealism seems in some way to justify the "realism" of common sense. But if the growth of positive knowledge and three centuries of reflective thought have served to rectify both this elemental realism and the philosophic realism which embodies it, they have not been able to overthrow the quite unexceptionable evidence on which this realism relies, wholly inseparable as it is from an idealist evidence which it would be wrong to neglect. For if it is certain that the object is in the first place a significance (or as some would say, an essence) and that it is intelligible only on that account, it follows that it acquires its status as being from moment to moment only by the thought which elicits such significance. Subject and object thus define together the situation of consciousness, which is such that its subjectivity cannot establish its own existence without introducing a world of objects and things which in turn cannot exist—that is, have meaning and value —apart from the subject which thinks them. On this view realism and idealism imply one another and cannot be separated or brought forward as rival "absolutes" without at the same time abolishing both the reality of consciousness as subjectivity and that of the world as objectivity. This it is, at bottom, which is signified by the medieval doctrine of the active intellect, the rôle of which is to "bring the intelligible into act". Without thought the universe waits, we may say, to be born; which is why Adam, according to Genesis (2. 19–20), was given by God the responsibility of naming both animals and things: to accord them a meaning, that is, and thus to confer upon them the actuality of being.

Realism and idealism, therefore, so far from being mutually exclusive, imply one another. Their union articulates the profoundest metaphysical truth about man—that he has been created by God in order himself to become a creator. For it is he who makes the *cosmos*, in the strict sense of the term as signifying order, unity and harmony. And this he does by means of his *word*—language and action together in the image and likeness of the divine Word. We may, then, conclude that it is only by recourse to God the creator that we can form any intelligible conception of the agreement and unity of thought and being and so reconcile the respective positions, equally necessary as they are and complementary, of realism and idealism. But we must now approach the problem of God by a different route.

THE PROBLEM OF GOD

We have seen that it is the very analysis of being as we experience it—an analysis fully contained in what we have called "metaphysical experience"—which reveals being to us as essentially finite and in process. Finitude and process are, in being, the effects of *composition*. Being appears, in fact, to be composed of (*a*) essence and existence, inasmuch as it is "something which exists"—that is something which is not itself existence but receives it; (*b*) act and potency, since being as experienced is never quite all that it is or could be and is always, so to speak, in pursuit of itself in order to achieve self-realization; and (*c*) substance and accidents—that is, having a kind of substratum of reality constantly undergoing modifications at the level of phenomena, of appearance.

It is this experience and analysis of being which leads us to ask whether the idea of a thing that would not, in all strictness, be *a* thing like all the others which we know or can imagine, but absolute Being—the plenitude and perfection of being—does not meet that demand for intelligibility in being which our experience forces upon us. A famous argument, known as the ontological, takes this very concept as its starting-point with a view to establishing the existence of an absolute Being—God—as a necessary implicate. St Anselm and Descartes, in slightly differing ways, sought to show its validity. Leibniz, too, accepted it in maintaining that if God is possible—if, that is, the concept of God involves nothing self-contradictory—then he exists necessarily. These arguments are not indeed acceptable as they stand. But if, as we have seen, being as we experience it is finite and contingent, from the very fact that both its structure and the process of becoming which it undergoes are evidence of its inherent poverty and incompleteness, we are bound to conclude that it is not self-explanatory and that while it has a reason for existing it is not itself that reason. It is upon this basis that the arguments for the existence of God as finite and necessary Being, Pure Act and the first and universal Principle of all that is or can be, inevitably rest.

We shall not dwell upon these arguments here, since they have been fairly fully developed elsewhere. But we must emphasize that what is called a "proof" of God's existence is less a proof, in the scientific meaning of the word, than the expression, in a technical and more or less complicated form, of an *intuition*—in the sense of a spontaneous and, in some sort, immediate inference—whereby every man, by virtue of the rational necessities which he cannot but admit, grasps in his experience of being itself a relationship to God which defines it and apart from which, as Sartre realizes, it would remain irremediably meaningless and absurd. The movement towards God, we would say, is as natural and spontaneous as breathing. We might even claim that it is the very breath of the spirit.

Nevertheless, this intuition needs to be made explicit and subjected to criticism, since it too easily yields to the charms and illusions of anthropomorphism. Such criticism should lead us to admit that if God is the absolute principle of everything that is or can be, he is, as such, absolutely transcendent of all that he brings into being. He himself, therefore, is not so much being as *Super-being*: without common measure, that is—however distant from us we may imagine him—with his creatures and absolutely exclusive of all such determinations as mark the objects of our own experience, or indeed of any sort of determination at all. And this too, despite the utter inadequacy of our images and concepts, is in some way contained in the spontaneous sentiment which every man has of

God as the absolute principle of all that is. But the rôle of metaphysics as a science is to enable us gradually to purify our ideas of divinity and to understand, moreover, that God is *par excellence* the infinite "Beyond", the absolutely "Other".

Yet this "Beyond", this "Wholly Other", is an actual *presence*, more immediately at hand than anything else, since, on account of its universally enfolding infinity and by means of its creative action—which causes everything at every moment to be what it is—it in some sort indwells each and every creature and is thus more truly present to them than they are to themselves. God is the act of all our moments, and if, so far as the senses are concerned, he is nothing, it is precisely because he is actually all things, just as, if he is nowhere, it is because he is everywhere.

Our contemporary thinkers—and notably, from differing points of view, Sartre and Merleau-Ponty—criticize this idea of God as "transcendence within immanence" if not as self-contradictory then at least as an empty notion, devoid of any experience which could give it meaning. In fact, they say, were one to attempt to conceive of God as he is in himself it would only be as the anonymous force which sustains each thought and each experience as it comes to us. But a foundation of this sort defies all analysis. Because I am not God the coexistence of transcendence and immanence (or presence) is bound to remain for me an unverifiable datum.

Such difficulties, however, are not decisive. For it is true that transcendence within immanence is something beyond any and every analogy, the plain fact being that I am not God and that God alone can fully express the truth of his being and action. But to demand that the mode of God's creative activity and the form of his presence in the world and in human consciousness should be "verifiable" in the same sense as that in which our mundane truths are verifiable is simply to lay down a condition which the problem excludes by definition and which, were it possible to fulfil it, would mean that our discourse did not in fact relate to God at all. Moreover, as we have already had occasion to point out, it would turn "verifiability" into a purely univocal idea such as would destroy, once and for all, not only all theological argument but every metaphysical concept whatsoever. Even positive knowledge would not escape, in so far as this too exceeds what is representable and verifiable.

The most general objection remains, however. "Neither the universe nor reason", we are told, "is in the last resort problematic. Say, if you will, that they are mysterious; but it is their mystery which defines them and there can be no question of dissolving it by some ready-to-hand 'solution'."[7] Now as to this we may observe, first, that if the universe and reason are "mysterious" by definition why should "transcendence within immanence" be disqualified on the score of mystery? But in going to the root of the objection we shall see that if the universe *as such* provides its own answer and can be sufficiently explained, in its *actual concrete being*, by means of science and philosophy—the identical hypothesis from which we set out in our discussion of positivism—it still does not account for *being as such*. "Why is there being rather than nothingness?" The question is so fundamental that it excludes all merely particular explanation of "this" in terms of "that"—in other words, all scientific explanation. The universe cannot answer it; or at any rate, if it does so it is only on condition that we ask it concerning that *being* whereby the universe is both what it is and what it becomes. We no doubt can refuse to entertain the problem; we can deny that the universe and reason are problematic. But to do so is the result of a decision. It is not a rational necessity.

It remains that recourse to God is not a "solution". God, surely enough, is the answer to our questionings, but not so as to put an end to "a certain point of tension"—to the

[7] Merleau-Ponty, *Phénoménologie de la Perception*, p. xvi.

disquiet that stimulates reflection and research. To believe in him is not to encourage a laziness of mind in which "ideas cease to multiply and live" and, "sinking to the level of mere excuses and pretexts", become but "relics and points of honour", "the sum of our nostalgic longings and resentments, our timidities and phobias".[8] The fear that belief might have this result is not idle: theism may and sometimes does turn into an intellectual soporific. But what ideas are there which are not exposed to a like danger? "The inherent problem presented by the world" can also become routine, a point of honour and a pretext. No idea is wholly exempt from misconception and abuse. But here it is the meaning and value of ideas which have to be considered. From this standpoint God is only very hesitantly to be spoken of as a "solution" of the problem offered by the universe; for this "solution" is of so special a kind—is, in truth, so far unique—that it excludes all comparison with our scientific and practical solutions. It is never such as to cause the problem of the world to disappear, since our affirmation of God's existence has at every moment to be remade in face of the uncertainties and deficiencies of reason and the beguiling attractions of visible things. Never does the "solution" abolish the problem; on the contrary, the latter must be taken up and considered afresh, again and again; the more so, indeed, as a "solution", once presented, itself gives rise to an endless series of new problems—is itself, in fact, the embodiment of a mystery which no amount of reflection will ever wholly remove. Recourse to God never dispenses us from the unending task (which is the joint task of science and philosophy) of understanding the world in which we are placed and of which we form a part—and first of giving it all its wealth of meaning; for such is truth's demand and man's responsibility. Whoever loses sight of the sheer strangeness of the universe, ceasing to ask questions about it and thus throwing aside that

[8] Merleau-Ponty, *Éloge de la Philosophie*, p. 63.

attitude of "doubt" which actually is no more than a needful alertness, loses thereby the sense alike of the universe, of man and of God.

There can be no question then, of *defining* metaphysics as atheism merely from the fact of its presenting itself as —in Merleau-Ponty's words—"the beginning of an attentive interest, of certain seriousness of mind, of an experience"; for such, even when theistic, it always essentially is. The affirmation of God, born at every moment of experience, attentive interest and sound reasoning, is the very form of the assent which we accord to the world itself, in overcoming the doubt inseparable from it in so far as the world fails to present us with a problem. Man is not truly metaphysical until he feels the need of combating the false gods of the imagination. For this kind of "atheism" is something which belief in God itself implies, the Saint being a "genuine atheist" as regards a deity who is only a guarantee of the natural order. And if such "atheism" is, historically, to be found in association with Christianity, yet it also is an expression of natural reason once the latter becomes aware of the anthropomorphism by which its concepts and thought-processes are inevitably permeated. For natural reason knows that the *via negativa* is the only really appropriate way to God and that nothing we may say about him is valid apart from this indispensable negative, not even the being which we attribute to him and which, in the sense which our experience gives it, is still a determination which cannot apply to him.

The mechanic–God or artificer–God, the geometrician–God of Leibniz, the world-ruler God of popular imagination —all such notions are doubtless no more inherently "absurd" than a great many other concepts which we make use of in trying to represent the first Principle and the universal Reason. It is only their particularity that makes them inadequate and invalid. For in regard to the divine everything may be of some use while nothing is of absolute validity. "How are we to speak of him?" asks Plotinus, "We indeed can speak of him, but we cannot say what he is in himself." Yet

> how can we speak of him if we cannot grasp him as he is in himself? The truth is that, although we cannot grasp him—as he is in himself—by knowledge, nevertheless we are not wholly unable to apprehend him. We have a sufficient apprehension of him to be able to speak of him, although our words cannot represent him as he intrinsically is. We can say what he is not; what he is we cannot say [for] we can speak of him only by speaking of things which are inferior to him.[9]

"The divine majesty," says Augustine to the same effect, "is so great that all that we affirm of it will always be unworthy of it, since in its ineffable grandeur it surpasses every resource of every tongue."[10] "Even the highest terms are yet so miserably inadequate that silence would be more truly respectful than any possible human word."[11] If God is a mystery—if he is the mystery of mysteries—then must we repeat, with St Thomas, that the purest knowledge of God is ignorance.

But in this case it is no longer a question of "atheism", but of asserting that the affirmation of God entails the negation of everything which is finite and imperfect in our concepts and expressions. "When we speak of God," says Gabriel Marcel, "it is not God of whom we speak."[12] The "negative way" described by St Thomas is not atheism but, on the contrary, a conscious and deliberate recognition on our part of how God stands in relation to our human thinking and speaking. But, it may be said, if this is so—if the idea of God entails a continuous critique of all our idols—"where can the final truth about God ever be said to reside?"[13] The answer doubtless is that this critique has, in fact, no assignable limits, inasmuch as we can never ultimately succeed in purging our

---

[9] *Enneads*, V, 8.

[10] *Contra Adimantum Manichaeum*, VII, 4.

[11] *Ibid.*, XI.

[12] *Du refus à l'invocation* (Paris, 1940), p. 53.

[13] Merleau-Ponty, *ibid.*, p. 65.

idea of God of all the impurities and imperfections which our finite human thought and imagination mingle with it. Who, from this point of view, could at any time flatter himself that he does know "where the truth about God resides"? God is infinite, and no representation or determination—nothing, indeed, that we can ever say about him—will suffice to express the whole meaning of his name. That is why the affirmation of God never implies a definitive or fully realized understanding of him. As a perpetual fresh start for a reason which, in the well-known words of St Augustine, seeks in order to find and finds only in order to seek yet again, God is never a "solution" in the sense that he simply puts an end to inquiry. More precisely, as the solution or answer to the problem of the meaning of life and the universe, God, both as he is in himself and in his relations with the world, is for our finite understanding the centre and ground of all questions.

CHAPTER VII

ETHICS AND AXIOLOGY

Problems of value occupy the whole field of what is called *morals (or ethics)* and *axiology* (or the *theory of values*). Here we have to consider problems of value in their strictly ethical aspect: that is to say, as they are posed for a conscience, distinguished absolutely from psychological consciousness (understood as merely the bare apprehension of interior facts), by which one acts not merely as a witness but as a legislator and judge whose task it is to decide what ought to be done here and now, and who recognizes an ideal of morality in regard to which he, as a moral subject, recognizes himself as personally responsible. It is this which we speak of as the moral fact; and it is characteristic of metaphysical man and as universal as the human species. Not that the human condition necessarily conforms to the laws of the moral order, for we know only too well that it does not; but it is certain that always and everywhere men have admitted, at any rate implicitly, the existence of moral values as something distinct from material values and have recognized themselves to be subject to moral laws setting forth an *ideal* of conduct and imposing the *duty* or the obligation of realizing in their lives, both individual and social, those values which merit unqualified respect—to the point indeed of its never having seemed possible to them to repudiate the demands of morality without at the same time repudiating their own humanity.

How are we to explain the phenomenon of morality? This is the basic problem which we have to examine. We have seen that the positive sciences cannot resolve it, any more than they can resolve the problems of existence and mind. But this is not conceded without discussion. We shall see that two kinds of theory are set in opposition to it: one which explains values as the arbitrary creation of man, and another which attributes the genesis of values to society as a whole. It will be our task, then, to study these two conceptions, both of which lead, though by differing routes, to the denial of the metaphysical character of man. Before doing so, however, it will be advisable to clarify the meaning of that natural law which is inherent in man, and which, as we interpret it, is another form of the presence of the Absolute.

THE NATURAL LAW

Under the name *natural law* we signify a law, known to us by the light of natural reason to be intrinsic to the nature of things, which derives from God as the author of nature and directs man's action to its ultimate end: namely, the perfection of his nature or the fulness of his humanity. Accordingly, natural law—or, as it is nowadays more commonly called, *natural right*—may be defined as a participation of the rational creature in the eternal law. For the creation of the universe appears as the realization of an eternal plan: a law, eternal as the divine mind itself, as unchanging as the divine wisdom, governs the entire universe and leads each and every individual being to the "end" demanded by its own nature and by its part and function in the whole. In inanimate beings it is a blind impulsion which is at work, the relation between end and means being purely mechanical. With the animal creation instinct is in control, thanks to which the natural law is fulfilled by the pressure of an internal necessity. In this case neither merit nor demerit, right nor duty, has any place. In man, however, natural law is not mechanical or instinctive, but *moral*. It binds the will, that is, but only in leaving to it a free choice as between good and evil; and it is from this, as we have seen, that man's moral responsibility is born. The moral law, therefore, is nothing other than the eternal law, in so far as the latter has as its object the regulation of human activity. Thus there is a radical difference between what conforms to the divine order and what opposes it—in a word, between good and evil. The ultimate order itself—the perfection of our humanity as such—appears as a law for the rational creature, in that it is essentially a divine order, a participation in the divine Reason.

The eternal law is, then, nothing less than God himself, who, through his Reason, governs all that he has created. We are, accordingly, a long way from the Stoic conception of law as a sort of impersonal decree (or Fate) to which even God himself is subject. In reality the eternal law, as we understand it, is bound up with the idea of creation and is inseparable from the Wisdom of God. That is why St Augustine and St Thomas tell us that God has "concreated" both the natural law and the beings which he called into existence. Hence we can describe the eternal law as in some sort "transcribed" or "inscribed" upon human reason: it is the divine Reason itself shining within us by way of participation. Precisely because of this, the natural law in man, endowed as he is with reason (however ill-instructed), comes to be identified with reason itself; for conscience, or, more exactly, the moral sense, is no more than this same reason as applied to the realm of action. Thus it is that the moral consciousness is coextensive, in fact as in principle, with the entire human race and properly defines man's nature.

From this ensue the moral law's essential characteristics. It is *obligatory*, in that it determines duty, though without impairing the freedom of the human will; *absolute*, in that it commands without any option; *universal*, as resting on and valid for the nature of all men without exception; and finally, *unchanging*, like the nature which provides its basis. Unless the primacy be given to the free play of instinct and brute force—apart, that is, from an eventual recourse to unlimited state sovereignty as a means of curbing the resulting anarchy

—we are bound to admit the reality of a higher norm founded upon nature and ultimately in the divin⸱ Reason. In what precisely the immutability of this fundamental law consists remains to be shown.

It would be a grave misrepresentation of the idea of natural right to conclude from its essential immutability that moral precepts are themselves absolutely unchanging and unchangeable. The truth is that the natural law itself varies and develops under forms and within limits which should be clearly grasped. We may, indeed, understand easily enough that if there is a sense in which the natural law is unchanging there also is another in which it must be seen as subject to change inasmuch as nature is itself both unchanging and everchanging. It is unchanging in its abstract essence, and by virtue of this we are able to establish its basic precepts— those which relate, that is, to man's fundamental tendencies and do not admit of modification under pressure of contingent circumstances (for the latter are the concern of what is called *positive law*). But nature is mutable and diverse in its concrete forms, both historic and individual. That is why natural law, in its more or less immediate applications, must constantly undergo adaptation, not so as to alter its substance, which of course cannot change, but in order, on the contrary, to assure its essential permanence. For example, the variations which, over the ages, are to be noted in the ethics of usury are explicable as so many adaptations to the concrete circumstances of economic and social life with a view to safeguarding the essential demands of justice. The law varies in order to secure its own permanence.

Furthermore we have to concede the reality of a general advance in man's knowledge of what in fact the natural law requires—that is, in his *intensive* understanding of it. It is in this that the progress of civilization, taken in its moral sense, really consists. Little by little humanity gains a more exact and lively awareness of certain aspects or consequences of the general principles of the natural law which hitherto had remained obscure or had come to light only in the form of utopias, or had been envisaged only by pioneers who were often misunderstood and persecuted. This explains the development brought about in the course of centuries in regard to slavery, the rules of war and the various forms of social justice. It is precisely this aspect of law that Bergson defined as an "open morality"—one, that is, which is always capable of further development as a result of a deepening knowledge of what the natural law itself prescribes and of a widening vision of its scope.

MORAL OBLIGATION

The moral law finds its essential expression in *obligation*—in the moral necessity which compels man either to do or to refrain from doing a given act, according to whether the natural law (or the positive law which determines or elucidates it) prescribes or forbids such an act. We now are in a position to understand the meaning and character of this moral necessity both as something that commands the will without forcing it—by reason of the very fact that it identifies itself with the will—and also as an absolute, in so far as it is an *unconditioned* necessity. It is not for us to *choose* our "end", since this is implicit in the human nature which we have received from God. Moral obligation, or duty, has as its immediate basis the intrinsic and necessary order of things in virtue of which there exists a necessary connection between this or that action and man's "end"—namely, the perfection of his nature. For its ultimate basis it has the ordinance of the divine creative Reason itself.

Attempts have been made, however, sometimes to explain the genesis of moral values without recourse to a law or an obligation, sometimes to reduce the sense of duty to the constraining force which society exercises over the individuals who compose it. We must submit both standpoints, therefore, to a brief examination.

There has been talk of "an ethic without obligation or sanction". This is the title of a work by Georges Guyau, published in 1885, which aptly summarizes the general drift of all theories which see in moral values only an arbitrary invention—theories which have of late been pertinaciously argued, from differing standpoints, by Sartre and R. Polin.[1] They tell us that value—whatever may be the object of our aims, desires or appreciation—constitutes a realm wholly distinct from being and gives rise to specific judgements through an evaluation which is essentially emotive and non-rational. Value, as thus understood, is inherently an ideal, a creation, a movement on man's part towards ends freely chosen but never "realized". Certain thinkers, Sartre among them, go so far as to maintain that on the basis of these principles the idea of moral values implies atheism, since in getting rid of the delusive image of a Being who would realize and therefore exhaust them, they compel us to posit, by the exercise of our freedom, ends which are capable of existing, in any concrete way, only in and for ourselves, the world of nature knowing nothing of them. Thus value has its ultimate foundation in the unlimited power of a freedom fully deployed and realized only in the act of choosing "ends"—i.e. values. But on this view, Sartre adds, freedom is absurd, since if the actual choice of values is itself the ground of the values chosen it is not the ground of choice itself, from which we can in no way withdraw ourselves. Always our "reasons" involve this fundamental absurdity, that freedom is the baseless basis of our valuations.

We cannot here discuss this theory at length, but because of the wide repercussions which it has had we should note the serious difficulties in the way of its acceptance. We shall not refer to the moral consequences which the Sartrean idea of freedom implies. They are sufficiently plain, and Sartre himself agrees that they necessarily exclude any morality

[1] J.-P. Sartre, *L'Être et le Néant*, p. 508 f., and R. Polin, *La Création des valeurs* (Paris, 1944).

envisaged as a rule of law or system of duties. But we wish to point out that if freedom as Sartre understands it is "absurd" it is so in a more radical sense than he admits. Indeed, it is a complete contradiction of the postulates of his doctrine, for according to these the *en-soi* (or being-as-it-is-in-itself) is absolutely exclusive of all relationship and of the *pour-soi* itself (i.e. consciousness). But, says Sartre, "everything happens as if the *en-soi*, in endeavouring to establish itself, were to acquire the character of the *pour-soi*". Yet this would amount to talking about an *en-soir-pour-soi*, which for him would be an utter impossibility. Sartre's idea of freedom is such, then, that to the intrinsic "absurdity" by which it is characterized it adds a radical contradictoriness within the system on which it rests.

On the other hand, Sartre affirms that if man, before being free—the word "before" having in this context a logical sense only and not a chronological one—possessed a "nature"or definite essence, this nature or essence would prove destructive of his freedom. But it is clear that this argument would be valid only if "essence" is always conceived—as, in fact, Sartre does conceive it—as identical with that of a material object. Actually, however, a finite essence is not at any time a wholly determinate and complete entity; there always is a certain indeterminateness or "give" about it. What it stands for in the case of man, contingent and free, is simply the "framework" within which a self-consistent development takes place. I can become *what* I wish to become within the framework of what I already am by nature; I can become *this* sort of person or that, but not a horse or a pebble! My freedom is unbounded within its limits, which act as such only in so far as they exclude what is self-contradictory and therefore impossible.

Sartre, however, by yet another twist of his peculiar logic, is able to invoke, in order to explain the genesis of values by the caprice of freedom, a *nature* or an *essence* that logically precedes existence. This consists (whatever may be the concrete and symbolic forms of its realization) in that "basic desire"—the desire, that is, to become God—which, in Sartre's view, characterizes the human state and which is already latent in the "framework" wherein existence has to manifest itself. Sartre here has committed himself to what is in effect a doctrine of human nature. The conclusion was in fact inevitable, and we do not reproach him, illogical though it is, with having reached it, but only with having absorbed it, so to speak, into a fallacious argument. It seems, then, that Sartre fails to give any really intelligible account of the genesis of values. But this does not mean that we propose to reject his teaching *en bloc*. We shall have to come back to it when we have examined the apparently contrary position of the sociological school.

Durkheim has seen clearly enough the difficulties of an ethic possessing neither obligation nor sanction and has tried to resolve them by locating the source of all values, and in particular of moral values, along with the feelings of obligation and duty which accompany and intrinsically qualify them, within society itself. This view, however, hardly appears compatible with another feeling no less vital to morals—namely, the sense of *autonomy*. But Durkheim, and others since, have believed it possible to avoid these embarrassments by explaining even this in terms of the social whole. A discussion of these theories, the influence of which has been and still is very far-reaching, will enable us the better to understand how here, too, as with the problems of being and mind, there is no valid solution save that which invokes the sole Absolute worthy of the name—and that is God. We shall see also that the feeling of autonomy and the demands of freedom clearly imply man's power of self-creation in the creation of his own values.

In his book on *Moral Education* Durkheim states as plainly as could be wished the problem of the genesis of this feeling of autonomy. "On the one hand", he writes, "moral rules appear to us, in view of all the evidence, as something external to the will. They are not of our making, so that, in submitting to them, we obey a law which we have not ourselves framed." We submit to a constraint which is none the less real for being moral. On the other hand, it is certain that the conscience protests against such dependence. We consider an act to be truly moral only when performed with complete freedom and under no compulsion whatever. Now we are not free if the law by which we regulate our conduct has been imposed upon us and without any free consent on our part. What solution does Durkheim bring, then, to the problem thus posed? It is, he says, science which will become the true source of our autonomy. For

> this [social] order which the individual, as an individual, has not created and has not deliberately willed can be made his own by science. The moral rules which impose themselves on us by authority can be investigated; their nature, their conditions (immediate or remote), and their aim and purpose can be discovered. In a word, we can reduce them to a science; and thus we are ourselves the masters of the moral realm. It has ceased to be something external to us, since it is revealed to us henceforth as a system of clear and distinct ideas whose relationship to one another we can grasp. Thus are we in a position to satisfy ourselves of the extent to which it is founded in the nature of things—i.e. in society—and hence of the degree of its obligatoriness. In so far as we are able to recognize this we can afford it our willing consent.[2]

The first thing to be said about this is that Durkheim's theory entirely fails to explain the emergence of morality. For the process which he describes itself *presupposes* morality; it does not give rise to it. Only a *moral subject* is capable of consenting to a moral order and of apprehending it as an "obligation". Instead of admitting the logical priority of this moral subject—and hence of morality itself—Durkheim, in striving to account for morality on a purely social basis, merely deludes himself, with the help of science, into

[2] *L'Éducation morale* (Paris, 1938) pp. 132 ff.

equating it with social conformism. "A conformism", he writes, "thus consented to has no element of restraint about it."[3] But the whole question is to see *how* a conformism of restraint can become one of consent, and above all how a conformism of consent can be a moral reality.

We must, in fact, first underline the ambiguity of the term "consent" as employed by Durkheim. For there are two ways of consenting: one which consists in submitting, by way of passive adaptation to the constraining force, and another which consists in *choosing*, in adopting and making our own the very law that imposes itself on us. Now it is not apparent how "science", that is, mere knowledge of the social mechanism, can of itself alone determine consent in the second of these two senses. It can only secure our submission to an order which transcends us and which we cannot escape, in much the same way as we adjust ourselves to cold or heat. How could it make us adjust ourselves *internally and actively*, not only as to something useful and (supposedly) beneficial, but also as to something *obligatory*, to a law which operates like a physical law? There seems to be no answer. So Durkheim has effected the transition from a "conformism of restraint" to a "conformism of consent" only by an equivocation.

Furthermore, even when "consented to" in the second sense, conformism would not be enough to account for the reality of morals. For the latter, strictly speaking, is not a matter of "conformism", even though consented to. It is, indeed, distinguished from anything purely social in that society itself is in some sort contained within the moral order as a function and expression thereof. Moreover, conformism is of no value in itself, but only by virtue of the moral principles on which it is based and through which it finds its justification. Unless it can appeal to such principles and to the rule of law it is of no value and ceases to belong to the realm of ethics. In Durkheim's meaning of the word conform-

[3] *Op. cit.*, p. 184.

ism signifies nothing other than sheer abandonment of the moral standpoint, "consent" here being equivalent to mere submission. In the long run there is only society and its demands, and these impose constraint whether consented to or not. In this context morality and obligation are but names.

G. Davy has shown himself well aware of the weaknesses of Durkheim's theory and has tried to strengthen it. His mistake, however, lies in supposing that a mere tightening up is enough, as though its essential principle were sound. As he sees it, the thing to do is to make good the point wherein, in his view—and here he is certainly right—Durkheim fails: namely, by showing that moral sentiments, once they are individualized, can achieve autonomy and acquire originality and effectiveness in transcending social existence. To establish this thesis Davy assumes that the collective consciousness produces by degrees an "ideal" which is the very form of morality and thereafter develops by its own power as an ethic distinct from and independent of the society in which it originated. This ideal, he adds, should be conceived as "a better conscience formed by the sharing of those ideas and aspirations to which association, by its ennobling power, gives rise".[4]

What Davy is here trying to do is no doubt well intentioned. He has a true enough idea of what the moral order ought to be, but unfortunately he is much less logical than Durkheim. Unless we are merely to be put off with words we are bound to ask what this "ideal" is, how it establishes itself as an ideal and whence it derives its obligatory force. Davy will not admit the control of a "super-will", conceived either as divine or as a norm superior both to society and to individual wills. His "ideal" can only be, therefore, a *collective ideal*; in other words, and conformably with the theory, a *quantitative* value and not a qualitative one—an expression simply of the mass. One fails, in fact, to see by what criterion one could rightly

[4] G. Davy, *Éléments de Sociologie*, I, p. 85. Cf. the same author's *L'idéalisme et l'expérience*, p. 161 f.

define and qualify it qualitatively—that is, morally—since to do that we should have to adopt a norm distinct from society. Otherwise the specific character of the "ideal" would derive from mass-pressure and would derive its value, not from its own content, but simply from the power of the collectivity which elaborates it. But this is only another way of saying that its "ideality" is in the end nothing but force or constraint. So we come back again, quite logically, to Durkheim.

For how can these common "aspirations", brought into being, as they are, by association, be transformed into an "ideal", and how can this ideal acquire the character of a self-authenticating moral obligation without reference to a norm of morality? That association, by its own ennobling strength, can engender a moral ideal is something not easily conceivable, for otherwise morality might well be shown to exist in the ant-hill, in a herd of cattle, or in a band of monkeys. There is no genuine "ideal" except for intelligent, free beings who for that very reason are moral, capable of seeing what *ought* to be above and beyond what *is* and of detecting justice behind the use of force. Were there not a "right" superior to mere "fact"—superior, therefore, to society simply as such—there would be neither ideal nor morality nor obligation.

Hence under whatever guise it presents itself the sociological theory fails to explain the genesis of moral values. It gives the appearance of explaining it and of being able to deduce morality from it only by gratuitously invoking facts— the moral standards of the group, the individual moral subject—which already imply it. The truth is that what is moral is not deducible from what is purely social; right is not to be derived merely from fact, for the two are heterogeneous. Society can, of course, become the vehicle and instrument of moral values, but it does not create them; for society itself depends upon them as much as does the individual conscience. The moral order is an order of right, encompassing society, justifying it and maintaining it. And this order is that of a reason which transcends the entire universe and which is not, therefore, to be explained save as a participation in the infinite Reason. God alone is above the world of fact, since the world of fact is of his own making. If, then, we can trace in society the expression of a law imposing itself on the conscience and so creating an obligation, it is because we discover in social existence the expression of an order which, in deriving from God, appears to us something infinitely wise and makes an absolute demand on our respect.

Durkheim's theory is, in reality, what he himself says it is: no more than an attempt to transfer to society the divine privilege of giving birth to Right and Duty. But no such attempt can succeed, for the ultimate reason that human society is not the Absolute. Constituting a moral whole which no doubt has, as such, a being distinct from the individuals who compose it, it has dignity and worth only as it becomes the instrument of personal values. Society is to be measured by man, whose ends it serves, not man by society. For man must be conceived of as a *person*, and hence as transcending both society and history. Otherwise he will be no more than a mere economic unit, a spiritually valueless atom, and in the end a pure abstraction.

THE CREATION OF VALUES

In opposing these theories we must not overlook the element of truth which they contain. For it is undoubtedly man himself—or society, through which he achieves self-expression—who creates moral values. The question simply is: In what does this creation consist?

It assuredly is not the work of society considered—as the sociological hypothesis requires that it should be—in its mere bulk or quantitative mass. There is nothing about it that is arbitrary, gratuitous or absurd, as Sartre claims, since man, in creating his values, shows himself obedient to an interior law (that is, "natural law") which also is the law of his own being, identifiable with himself as a rational and free entity. There are thus two dangers to avoid: that of asserting that values pre-exist in things and that man has only to take possession of them; and that of claiming that the genesis of values is a pure invention of man's own, having no other ground than a choice which in fact is groundless. Consequently the problem is that of explaining the inner law from which values derive; in other words, of explaining man himself. And this plainly involves the "whole man" as a metaphysical being, and indeed all metaphysics.

Sartre's solution, which proceeds on a clear understanding of the problem itself, consists in explaining, if we may so put it, the absurdity of freedom and value by the still more fundamental absurdity of the "human reality", arising—why or how cannot be said—in the very heart of being, which is itself massive, opaque and compact. This it is which Sartre calls "the great adventure of the *en-soi*."[5] But can we describe it as a solution? For what we have here is nothing more than a logic—a logic of the "absurd", the most cumbersome of all postulates. We shall maintain that it certainly is "reason", that is, man, which (or who) has to provide the basis of the whole scheme of our values, including morality; and also that, as Nietzsche puts it (supposing—wrongly—that this involved "the death of God"), "man is the creator and nurturer of values", and that "a virtue must needs be *our* invention, *our* defence, *our* personal *necessity*". But this invention, choice or necessity, cannot be reduced, save at the cost of forfeiting all meaning and becoming wholly "absurd", to a mere game of chance, and a development out of nothingness. It has somehow to be accorded a proper basis and a justification. This is what Kierkegaard made so abundantly plain in his long polemic against Kant.[6] For the invention of values, he declares, is intelligible only as a response to a "call from on high"—only, that is, if it is the act by which, in assuming

[5] *L'Être et le Néant*, p. 269.
[6] *Journal*, VII A 181; VIII A 185; X2 A 428; X3 A 618.

the spiritual nature given us from God, we realize by our own free effort the true meaning of that nature. In one of its aspects this call is assuredly a sort of "constraint"—to which we assign the name of *moral obligation*—since it derives from a nature that is *given* to us; but it is a "constraint" which does not constrain: for on the one hand, while hearing it, I can act as though I did not do so, and on the other, in so far as I fear and obey it, I am put in possession (in freely becoming what I am) of the profoundest truth about myself. "I have nothing," writes Blondel,

> which I have not received. Yet at the same time everything has to come from me, including even the being which I have received and which appears to have been imposed upon me. No matter what I do or endure, I have always to sanction that being and create it, as it were, anew by a personal commitment, without my will, at its deepest and truest, ever really disavowing it.[7]

The whole of our moral experience shows us that the *actual self*, as it exists here and now in its concrete individuality, at grips with its particular problems and tirelessly inventing its own values, is in some sort sustained by the *ideal self* voiced in the appeal arising from the depths of one's nature so that it thus becomes one with the universal. It is ethics which furnishes us with the fullest proof of this miracle of an invention which is also a discovery, of a freedom which is also a condition of obedience, of a choice which is also self-choice, whereby the universal subsists in the particular without either destroying or diminishing it. The existent is, in fact, the coincidence or the unity of the universal and the particular or unique, both in the moral and in the rational order. Consciousness can exist only as a function and as the unity of the particular and of the universal; its experience at the pre-reflective and spontaneous level already implies both of men. It is simultaneously consciousness of the self and of other beings as sharing in the

[7] *L'Action* (1893), p. xxiv.

same objective universe, rational, moral and spiritual. Nothing, therefore, prevents us from saying that the metaphysical subject (that is, the person) is properly the centre of all things and that the whole, both as a world of things and as a universe of persons, is built up around the metaphysical subject. For that in no sense takes away from the essential universality which defines it as a *metaphysical* subject, but presupposes and requires it. This is what Sartre fails to see, so that he has been led to identify the metaphysical centre with a *psychological* one, this in turn becoming a sphere of egoism and strife, or of what he himself calls "the conflict of transcendences"; whereas the metaphysical subject, being a unity of the particular and the universal, is intrinsically a source of harmony and communion, of generosity and peace.

We thus rediscover, under a new aspect and by another route, the conclusion, which we adumbrated at the start in regard to the absolute. In truth there is nothing greater in the world than the freedom by which man can achieve "an equation of the reflective and the spontaneous movements",[8] an equation, that is to say, of the self with the self. It is indeed one of the three wonders wherein Descartes, in his youthful enthusiasm, perceived the absolute forms of the divine generosity: "Creation *ex nihilo*, free will and God made man."[9]

We talk too glibly about Morality—with a capital M—as though the entire system of our obligations and duties existed prior to man himself. Actually nothing pre-exists in this way, unless it be the *human nature* which defines man (and is prior to him only in a logical sense) and which simply is one with what we have already characterized as the "natural law" —this again being nothing other, essentially, than reason itself and that *demand of morality* (or of humanity) which is what reason really signifies. It is on the basis of this demand of nature that man has to create the values by which he

[8] M. Blondel, *L'Action* (1893), p. xiv.
[9] *Cogitationes privatae* (ed. Adam & Tannery), X, p. 228.

increasingly achieves self-fulfilment, both in his historical existence and in his personal individuality. Human history is the boundless field of the laborious effort whereby man, in creating values, *makes himself starting from himself* and so becomes truly what he is. This process of creation or invention is necessarily to be found in every individual life, since each person, in order to acquire a moral character, must draw from his own inner being the values that history has developed—as though, from the demand for reason and morality which defines him and which indeed he *is*, humanity itself were to have its beginning in him all over again. He also must strive to promote, for the good of the whole, that *conquest of the human* which is our true and only destiny. All of this, in the end, means nothing else than man's freedom, along with the responsibility which is bound up with it; for freedom can be understood only by reference to this continuous invention—ever resumed and pursued afresh—of the moral values by which man's humanity is realized.

That is why we can say, without paradox, that there is no such thing as "Morality", or that morality is simply the living consciousness which man possesses of his free, rational nature as coming to him from the Absolute to which that same nature feels itself drawn more and more urgently by love, for, as Sartre himself has observed, the profoundest truth about man, his true nature, is his hunger for God. It is all this which, with Kierkegaard, we should describe as "the call from on high", or, as it is still commonly termed, "the voice of conscience"—the source of man's moral genius as we see it ever at work in the creation of values. But if there is no such thing as "Morality", neither are there moral values subsisting of their own independent power. There is only one Law—that, namely, of the human person—and it is from it that, gradually, hazardously and painfully, the entire system of man's duties and obligations is derived and developed. Hence it really is man who invents and creates values as a response to that call from on high which is no other than a call for his self-realization in accordance with the ideal of his own nature. And by the same token *man creates himself* in the sense that he becomes more and more clearly conscious of what he is—as also of what he has to become so as to be truly and fully what he is. The history of mankind, if it has a meaning at all—if it is more than a mere "tale told by an idiot"—is but the progressive, laborious and tumultuous bringing to birth, simultaneously and inseparably, of man and his values. History, too, is metaphysical.

Thus also the problem of the *transcendence of values* takes on a new and much less contentious aspect. On the one hand, indeed, the transcendence of values is nothing else than the transcendence of man himself as reason and spirit, these finding their expression and fulfilment in his metaphysical dimension. On the other hand, the transcendence of man is real and thinkable only because he is a creature of God whose vocation in this world is to bring about, through faith and love, that *relation to God* in which his being has its deepest and truest meaning. From this point of view the progressive invention or creation of moral and spiritual values is at the same time the *humanization and divinization* of man, since by them—in realizing his humanity—he realizes more and more that likeness to God which defines his origin and his destiny, a likeness which the mystery of grace makes possible far beyond any hope and ambition of his own. Lastly, if God is infinite Value, or, more precisely, the *Super-value*, the source of all values, then man, in relating himself to God, becomes himself the sum and truth of all mundane values.

CONCLUSION

Metaphysics, in the fullest and most general sense of the word, appears as a permanent attempt of the human mind, confronted by its manifold experience, historical and individual, of being, thought and value, to be at one with an Absolute which itself impels us from within by its creative presence. Thus envisaged, metaphysics is no longer the vocation of a cultivated few. It is to be found everywhere, in life and in thought, in science and in religion, in institutions and in techniques, in civilizations and in cultures. For nothing ever wholly escapes the metaphysical demand, the metaphysical impulse. Misconceived or denied, our "metaphysical need" merely *absolutizes* the provisional and partial stages, instruments or expressions of the sole Absolute and so nourishes an idolatry unworthy of our humanity. Human life, says Blondel, is always and necessarily "a metaphysic in act"; we can evade metaphysics only by becoming something less than human. In fact, every question about man and the universe takes on a metaphysical character the moment it raises the problem of ends, and ceasing to lose itself in the objectivity of mechanisms and natural laws turns to the question of *meaning*—so soon, that is, as it moves on from description to understanding.

For metaphysics looks essentially to what gives to all things their ultimate significance. Hence recourse to the Absolute of meaning is implied in all its phases and makes it what properly it is: first at the level of ordinary life, then (and indissociably) at that of reflection and analysis. This movement towards, or quest of and search for, meaning, this demand for the Absolute, is the supreme characteristic of mind, or, as some might prefer to put it, of the reason as spirit—for there is a "reasoning" reason, labouring away at its abstractions, which is never more than an instrument of spirit. Spirit, then, is inherently determined by this need which exists within it as the very "presence" of the Absolute.

Thus it is possible to say, with profound truth, that "unless we already drew our being from God we could never realize God in us"[1]—could never, in other words, by reflective thinking actualize within us the idea of God. But it also is true that God, as both the source of all meaning and the principle of our understanding, is himself beyond comprehension; and this being so, even for metaphysics the ultimate Origin —which is contemporaneous with every instant of time, since it is only moving things which have to make continual fresh starts—remains a mystery.

From this point of view the phenomenon of metaphysics cannot, strictly speaking, be self-explanatory; it cannot, that is, be stated in terms of non-metaphysical causation. It has its beginning in metaphysical man—in the mind which expresses it, as best it can, by means of representations and concepts which aim at formulating, albeit in a way necessarily inadequate, that relation to the Absolute which provides its own essential definition. That is why we have said that metaphysics begins of itself and yet indefinitely precedes itself. It resists all attempts to destroy it by criticism since it cannot be other than a reflection, whether spontaneous or deliberate, upon the metaphysical phenomenon of man himself and because his relationship to the Absolute is the essence of his humanity, which can be impaired by nothing.

This relation to the Absolute, which metaphysics as a form of systematic knowledge gradually brings to light on the basis of our living experience and which appears more and more as the presence of God to the consciousness, naturally assumes a religious aspect which, however, finds complete expression only in positive religions. That is why it is so difficult, as a matter of historical fact, to separate metaphysics from religious

[1] Lagneau, *Célèbres leçons* (Paris, 1950), p. 301.

faith. Nevertheless, it is essential to distinguish them, as St Thomas has shown,[2] by reason of their respective sources, which in the case of metaphysics is the natural reason (or mind) and, in that of religion, Revelation. But the fact is that religion, in its concrete historical reality, includes or implies the whole of metaphysics and that metaphysics in one way or another has need of religion in order to acquire its full meaning and practical value; which amounts to saying that it really invokes Revelation, inasmuch as "man", in St Thomas' words, "is destined to attain to God" not only as he may be known by natural reason "but still more as he transcends our natural understanding"[3], that is, as he is in himself. Metaphysics, in so far as it embodies and elicits our relation to God the creator, the absolute and absolutely transcendent principle of universal being in all its modes, actual or possible, provides at its own level the basis of religion, in supplying it with the rational foundation necessary for its establishment. But religion likewise, in relating us to the God of revelation and the order of supernature, gives in its turn a necessary solidity and force to metaphysics by lifting it from the plane of the merely abstract and rational to that of life as a whole.

It could be said, therefore, that "philosophy and religion alike embrace the totality of our life", that "they have the same content", but that "they do not have the same form," the one being theoretical and the other practical.[4] This view, however, although perfectly sound as far as it goes, needs supplementation. For if religion is essentially a matter of practice it yet contains a cognitive element, at least "figuratively and enigmatically", that of faith in supernatural mysteries, and also the rational understanding which serves as its basis. On the other hand, if metaphysics is essentially speculative, it already implies, at least in the moral order, a

[2] *Summa Theol.*, Ia, qu. i, art. 6.
[3] *Op. cit.*, Ia, qu. i, art. 1.
[4] H. Duméry, *Critique et Religion* (Paris, 1957), p. 23.

practical need and a certain attitude to life. Hence the relation to the Absolute is never wholly confined to the metaphysical plane of pure reason and tends as a rule to express itself, when its exigencies are fully realized, in the context of a positive religion. It is in this sense that metaphysics is religious, not as a so-called "natural religion", which in fact is no more than an abstraction having neither historical reality nor practical value, save within a positive religious faith which both envelops it and fulfils it.

The paradox of our present-day civilization, geared as it is to the demands of technological progress, lies in the belief that it can survive without regard for metaphysics, or, consequently, for religion. But is this possible, since it is evident that a technological civilization has not and cannot have its regulative principle within itself? Lacking all metaphysical sense, closed to any intimation of the supernatural and the mysterious, it is moved and guided only by a "will to power", now inspired to boundless ambition, now unnerved by dread of things to come. If humanity is to survive it must once more learn what man himself is; it must recover its sense of man. Obsessed with his techniques, deprived of the support of those natural communities which humanize his relationship to the world around him, befogged by abstract and conflicting notions, beset by excitement and noise, assaulted by an ever-increasing barrage of propaganda, and appalled by the very idea of the solitude which makes sober reflection possible and in which the individual, who alone in the long run exists, can take account of himself and of his spiritual destiny, and seeking, finally, a way of escape in the pseudo-faiths of "progress" and "history"—and without even trying to reconcile them—modern man no longer lives in accordance with his true measure but is the victim of the relentless mechanism which he has fashioned with his own hands and can no longer control. At the same time he is losing all sense of human values and of the hierarchical order which commands them.

In truth, however, the metaphysical sense is never wholly lost. Like a river which seems to disappear into the ground and then reappears further on without interruption of its course, and not seldom with a fresh access of vigour, it does not cease, though forgotten or denied, to recapture man's attention, always (and increasingly) dissatisfied as he is even in the midst of his most spectacular material successes. The human race feels instinctively that its destiny is not achieved simply by controlling the earth and securing a universal and supposedly complete realization of physical comfort. The anxiety with which our contemporary civilization and its mass-culture are permeated through and through reminds the men of today, at least from time to time, that they have either a metaphysical meaning or none at all; for neither economics nor technology, neither politics nor sociology, is of worth except as it promotes human values in view of the eventual coming of the Man who is man indeed—of him who is yet more than man, in whom all this world's values find their focus and their complete fulfilment.

GLOSSARY OF TERMS

(including those marked * in the text)

Analogy. A relationship established between realities essentially different but yet having something in common (e.g. between *truth* and *light*, so that we can speak of "the light of truth").

Analytic. *Analytic judgement*: one in which the predicate is implied in the idea of the subject itself and can be drawn from it by analysis (e.g. when we say that "a circle is round").

Anthropomorphism. A way of thinking which extends to other beings what properly is characteristic of man alone. Esp. in applying to God attributes found in man only in an imperfect and defective condition.

A priori. Whatever is conceived or affirmed by logical necessity (e.g. "Man is free", freedom being a consequence of the possession of reason; or "God is just", justice belonging necessarily to a perfect Being).

Categories. The ultimate kinds or primary divisions of being (substance, quality, quantity, relation, time, place, situation, action, passion, possession). In Kant, the fundamental *a priori* concepts (as resulting, that is, from subjective necessity) of pure reason.

Conceptualization. The act of translating an experience or intuition in concepts (i.e. in an abstract and general form).

Contingence. The character of that which does not in and of itself possess the sufficient reason for its existence.

Determination. Mode of being.

Determinism. A postulate according to which all existing things constitute a single and univocal whole whose elements, universally and absolutely interdependent, are subject in space and time to the control of an absolute necessity.

Empirical, Empiricism: a tendency of thought, common to both sensualism and phenomenalism, which holds that all knowledge is finally reducible to sense-data.

Epiphenomenalism. The theory of being which regards consciousness as no more than an *epiphenomenon* (i.e. a mere "reflection" of organic activity).

A priori forms. For Kant: the laws by which thought, from its
own internal structure, organizes experience and builds up
systematic knowledge.

Immanence. Immanent: that which is internal to anything.

Intelligibility. Intelligible: that which is capable of being explained, on whatever grounds.

Intentionality. The quality of having a definite sense or purpose;
or, alternatively, of being dependent on or pointing to another term (e.g. Consciousness is always consciousness *of*
something, never merely consciousness pure and simple).

Transcendental logic. For Kant: the body of laws resulting from
the interaction of *a priori forms* (see above).

Metempirical. That which is beyond sense-experience as such,
but which nevertheless still belongs to the realm of nature
(e.g. time, space, causality, finality).

Mysticism. The *mystical state*: the state in which the soul enters
into direct or experimental relation with God. At its highest
it is a form of ecstasy.

Necessary. In an *absolute* sense: that which is unable not to be
(i.e. which exists of its own essence). In this sense God alone
is necessary. *Relatively*: that which cannot *not* be, or exist
in a manner other than that in which it does, within or under
certain conditions.

Phenomenon. Whatever appears to sense or to consciousness.

Phenomenological. That which relates to the descriptive study of
a phenomenon or group of phenomena as given in experience and presented in their objective being.

Relativism. A doctrine which argues the relativity of all knowledge (which considers it, that is, as incapable of attaining
to truth—scepticism—or else as incapable of attaining the
absolute—Kantian "critical" philosophy or positivism).

Solipsism. The extreme outcome of idealism, being the view that
the individual self (together with the whole scheme of his
representations) is alone creative of the real.

Synthetic, Synthetic a priori judgement: In Kant, a judgement in
which the predicate adds something to the idea of the subject

(i.e. realizes a synthesis), but does so in a way purely *a priori*, in virtue of the *a priori* forms of the pure understanding.

Transcendence, Transcendent. In general, that which pertains to whatever is above and beyond a given order of reality (as when, e.g., the soul is said to transcend the body, or a concept to transcend an image). In an *absolute* sense: that which pertains to what is above and beyond all reality and all actual or possible orders of reality—the Transcendence, in a word, which belongs to God alone.

Transcendental. In Kant: a concept not founded on any intuition and thus absolutely *a priori*.

Univocal. Univocal concept: whatever can be attributed identically to different subjects (e.g. the concept "man" as applied to Peter, Paul, a white man or a black).

SELECT BIBLIOGRAPHY

The classical metaphysical texts include the seventh book of Plato's *Republic* and the same author's *Phaedo* and *Theaetetus*, Aristotle's *Metaphysics*, the *Enneads* of Plotinus (Book V), St Thomas Aquinas' *On Being and Essence*, Descartes' *Metaphysical Meditations*, Malebranche's *Dialogues on Metaphysics*, Leibniz' *Discourse on Metaphysics*, Kant's *Critique of Pure Reason* and Hegel's *Phenomenology of Mind*. Among the more important modern texts are Heidegger's *What is Philosophy?* and *Introduction to Metaphysics* and Sartre's *Being and Nothingness*.

In this series: Delhaye, Philippe: *Christian Philosophy in the Middle Ages*; Nédoncelle, Maurice: *Is there a Christian Philosophy?* Trethowan, Illtyd: *The Basis of Belief*.

COLEBURT, R.: *An Introduction to Western Philosophy*, London and New York, Sheed and Ward, 1958.

COPLESTON, F. C.: *Contemporary Philosophy*, London, Burns and Oates, and Westminster, Md, Newman Press, 1956; *Aquinas*, Harmondsworth and Baltimore, Penguin Books, 1955.

EMMET, D.: *The Nature of Metaphysical Thinking*, London, Macmillan, and New York, St Martin's Press, 1945.

EWING, A. C.: *Fundamental Questions of Philosophy*, London and New York, Macmillan, 1951.

GILSON, Etienne: *God and Philosophy*, New Haven, Conn., Yale Univ. Press, 1941; *The Unity of Philosophical Experience*, London and New York, Sheed and Ward, 1938.

HAWKINS, D. J. B.: *Being and Becoming*, London and New York, Sheed and Ward, 1953; *Crucial Problems of Modern Philosophy*, London and New York, Sheed and Ward, 1957.

HEIDEGGER, M.: *Existence and Being*, London, Vision Press, 1950, and Chicago, Regnery, 1951.

LEWIS, H. D.: *Our Experience of God*, London, Allen and Unwin, 1959.

LOEWENBERG, J.: *Reason and the Nature of Things: Reflections on the Cognitive Function of Philosophy*, La Salle, Ill., Open Court, 1959.

MacIntyre, A. (Editor): *Metaphysical Beliefs*, London, S.C.M. Press, 1957.

Marcel, G.: *The Mystery of Being*, London, Harvill Press, 1950, and Chicago, Regnery, 1951; *Metaphysical Journal*, London, Rockliff, 1952.

Maritain, J.: *A Preface to Metaphysics*, London and New York, Sheed and Ward, 1939.

Mascall, E. L.: *Existence and Analogy*, London and New York, Longmans, 1949.

Paton, H. J.: *The Modern Predicament*, London, Allen and Unwin, and New York, Macmillan, 1955.

Pears, D. F. (Editor): *The Nature of Metaphysics*, London, Macmillan, and New York, St Martin's Press, 1957.

Pontifex, Mark, and Trethowan, Illtyd: *The Meaning of Existence*, London and New York, Longmans, 1953.

Ramsey, I. T. (Editor): *Prospect for Metaphysics*, London, Allen and Unwin, 1961.

Tomlin, E. W. F.: *Living and Knowing*, London, Faber, and New York, Harper, 1955.

Trethowan, Illtyd: *An Essay in Christian Philosophy*, London, Longmans, 1954.

Versfeld, M.: *Mirror of Philosophers*, London and New York, Sheed and Ward, 1960.